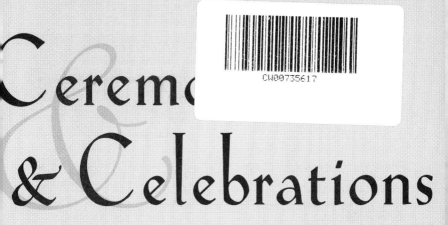

Ceremonies & Celebrations

VOWS, TRIBUTES AND READINGS

Dally R. Messenger

hachette
AUSTRALIA

This edition is dedicated to *Lois D'Arcy*,
the first celebrant appointed in Australia, and
Lyn Knorr the second celebrant

All editions of this book are dedicated to *Mr Justice Lionel Murphy*,
the founder of the world's first independent civil celebrancy, a great
statesman, a great Australian; to *Marjorie Messenger* and *Rick Barclay*,
Mary Hancock, and to *Dr Fred Klarberg*.

hachette
AUSTRALIA

Published in Australia and New Zealand in 2008
by Hachette Australia
(an imprint of Hachette Australia Pty Limited)
Level 17, 207 Kent Street, Sydney NSW 2000
www.hachette.com.au
10 9 8 7 6 5 4 3

First published in 1978, privately, as *Cultural Celebrations* in Australia; then
published in 1979 by Brian Zouch Publications Pty Ltd as *Ceremonies for Today*
Reprinted 1979
2nd edition published in 1984 by Dove Communications
3rd edition published in 1992 by Dally M. Publishing and Research Pty Ltd
4th edition published in 1999 by Thomas C. Lothian Pty Ltd
Reprinted 2003, 2004

Copyright © Dally R. Messenger 1999

National Library of Australia
Cataloguing-in-Publication data:

Messenger, Dally R. (Dally Raymond).
    Ceremonies & celebrations: vows, tributes and readings.

    Bibliography.
    Includes index.
    ISBN 978 0 7336 2317 2

    1. Rites and ceremonies – Australia. 2. Marriage service – Australia. 3. Funeral
    service – Australia. 1. Title.

392.0994

Text design by Jo Waite
Cover design by saso content & design Pty Ltd
Cover image: Copyright © Elena Elisseeva
Back cover photo: Dally R. Messenger (Karen Phillips)
Illustrations: IPL Image Group-Superstock: Julia McLeish; Denica Wapshott
Printed in Australia by Griffin Press

PEFC

PEFC/COC-0594

Contents

Acknowledgements

I wish to thank the following for permission to publish poetry, verse and quotations: Bryce Courtenay, extract from *A Recipe for Dreaming*, Reed Books, Port Melbourne; e. e. cummings, 'love', from *Complete Poems*, MacGibbon & Kee Ltd/Granada Publishing Ltd, St Albans, Herts; Kate Fisher, 'Now We Are One'; Kahlil Gibran, excerpts from 'On Children', 'On Death', 'On Friendship', 'On Love' and 'On Marriage' from *The Prophet*, Random House Inc., New York; Michael Leunig/*The Age*, excerpt from the Curly-Pyjama letters; Rod McKuen, verse from works published by W. H. Allen & Co. Ltd, London; James McCauley, extract from poem, University of Arkansas Press; Gloria Matthew, 'Marriage Is Love', 'Marriage Lines' and 'Memories and Peace'; 'Song', by Oodgeroo of the tribe Noonuccal (formerly known as Kath Walker), in *My People*, 3rd edn, 1990, published by Jacaranda Press; Walter Rinder, *Love Is an Attitude*, copyright 1970, Celestial Arts, Berkeley, Calif.; Stanley Sewell, 'The Giving'; Sheil Land Associates Ltd, for Pam Ayres, 'Yes, I'll Marry You, My Dear'; Rabindranath Tagore, 'Bless This Little Heart' and 'Where Have I Come From' from *The Crescent Moon*, 'On the Day When Death' and 'I Was Not Aware' from *Gitanjali*, and 'Let Thy Love Play' from *Crossing*, by permission of the trustees of the Tagore Estate and Macmillan, London; Dylan Thomas, extract from *Under Milk Wood*, J. M. Dent, London; Brian Zouch, 'To a Marriage' and 'To My Wife', and for being the original force behind *Ceremonies for Today*.

For this fourth edition, my deepest thanks to Carol Astbury, Lucia and Daniel Blums, Joyce Edmonds, Mary Hancock, Kathy Hurley, Vic and Jay Kennedy, Lyn Knorr, Des and Jennifer Lambert, Ted Logan, Genevieve Messenger,

Marjorie Messenger, Mark Miller and Sylvia Grobtuch, Liana Preston, and Martin Reilly, for permission to use photos, ceremonies or parts of ceremonies.

I also wish to thank the following for assistance, contributions and suggestions for the previous editions: David Atkins, Rick Barclay, Kath Buttriss, Sheree da Costa, Dawn Dickson, Leonie Hill, Max Howard, Lydia Kolomoicev, Brian McInerney, Jurgen Malina, Rachel Messenger, Janet Morice, Benjamin and Marlene Parer, Thomas Parsons, Beverley Pascoe, June Pellegrino (National Library), Geoff Potts (Attorney-General's Department), Bruce Shand, Beryl Shaw, Amanda Stephens, Rex Thompson, Colin and Marie Watson, Catie Wood, and Elizabeth Woodburn.

Disclaimer

Every effort has been made to trace and acknowledge all original source material contained in this book. The author and publisher would be pleased to hear from authors or publishers in order to rectify any errors or omissions.

Part 1

WEDDINGS

1 Your Wedding

Organising
Your Wedding Ceremony

Step 1

When you decide to have a wedding ceremony with a celebrant, how do you find one?

- Enquire among your friends and acquaintances. It is easy to find someone who can recommend a celebrant who does the task well.
- Consult the guidelines for choosing a celebrant on www.collegeofcelebrancy.edu.au – the College of Celebrancy's website – or other non-commercial celebrant sites. Bear in mind there is a wide disparity of professional standards betweeen celebrants.

There are excellent celebrants, and there are unsatisfactory celebrants. Your wedding ceremony is the most important part of your day, and it is important that you find a professional celebrant who will work with you, prepare, rehearse, and officiate at a really beautiful ceremony in accordance with your wishes. The ceremony component is probably the lowest cost of your whole wedding, so why spoil your day to save a few dollars? The Federation office will give you guidelines on fees.

Step 2

Contact a celebrant to discuss the type of ceremony you want, and the availability of the celebrant for the time and place you wish. All being well, you and the celebrant arrange to meet each other at a mutually convenient time, usually at the celebrant's home or office.

Step 3

The celebrant then posts to you a government form, the *Notice of Intended Marriage*, together with a request for other particulars; alternatively, you complete this at the meeting with the celebrant. The *Notice of Intended Marriage* must be lodged with the celebrant one month and one day before the wedding date. Mothers' maiden names are required, and the years of birth of children of any previous marriages.

As well as the particulars on the *Notice* each party should show the celebrant proof of birth (e.g. extracts of birth), passports or naturalisation certificates.

Where there has been a previous marriage, you must provide evidence of how it ended, usually a Decree Absolute in the case of a divorce, or a death certificate if a previous partner has died.

Step 4

You then meet the celebrant by arrangement. In addition to the *Notice of Intended Marriage*, you may then give the celebrant a copy or a first draft of the proposed ceremony, printed or neatly written on small sheets of paper (A5, about the size of this book) or on disk, the given names by which you wish to be called during the ceremony, and the exact time and address of the place for the marriage.

This is the best time to discuss any details regarding the arrangements, and to get to know the celebrant.

Step 5

The celebrant and the wedding party should meet for a rehearsal, preferably at the place of the marriage, or some other suitable venue.

Step 6

On the day, and at the place and time arranged, all parties, including the guests, meet and the marriage takes place.

Help Your Celebrant Do a Good Job

CHOOSING A CELEBRANT

The one big advantage to the community in the civil celebrant programme is that you can choose your celebrant. Celebrants are not confined to areas. Different celebrants suit different people; not all celebrants are the same, and they differ in their approach. All celebrants should give you complete choice of ceremony.

If you cannot decide on a celebrant — by seeing one conducting another marriage ceremony or by personal recommendation — one way to find someone suitable without inconveniencing people is to make a phone call. Ask what the celebrant's procedure is for choice, consultation, planning, rehearsal and ceremony. If this is satisfactory to you, then ask about the celebrant's availability on the day and time you require.

BOOKING A CEREMONY

When ringing a good celebrant, have ready a list of several alternative times for your ceremony. The best celebrants are usually booked well in advance for the most popular times, and alternative times give you a greater choice of celebrants. Almost everyone wishes to be married at 5 p.m. on a Saturday afternoon, so do not be surprised if this time is not available to you at short notice.

FILLING IN FORMS

As I have already said, before the ceremony you must complete the *Notice of Intended Marriage*.

The celebrant may also have a form for the details you require for your ceremony.

AT THE FIRST INTERVIEW

If you have all your documents prepared in advance, you can spend the time with the celebrant discussing the details that concern you, and getting to know your celebrant as a person. It is also more convenient to pay the fee at this time.

On the matter of fees, a warning! You pay least for cask wine, a bit more for a cheap bottle, a bit more for something reasonable, a bit more for the best. Beware of cheap celebrants.

WRITING TO THE CELEBRANT

Sometimes it is necessary to write or send a fax or an e-mail to a celebrant, especially when an interview is not possible or documents for the ceremony, which were not available at the time of the interview, have to be forwarded. Observe a golden rule here: always quote the date and time of your ceremony, as well as your names, as most celebrants file their papers in date and time order.

THE CEREMONY ITSELF

Marriages take place in all sorts of places — reception centre chapels, hotel wedding rooms, church buildings, former churches or multi-purpose ceremony centres, special function rooms of restaurants, parks and gardens, beaches, mountains, yachts, and private homes — you name it.

Having officiated at many marriages I can say with absolute certainty that no matter where a marriage ceremony takes place, people take the ceremony very seriously. The celebrant or master-of-ceremonies should ask people to put down their drinks and butt out their cigarettes before the ceremony starts.

Do not embarass your celebrant and your guests by choosing a ceremony that is too short. The ceremonies in the next chapter are the minimum length.

Always have a table or similar piece of furniture cleared for the celebrant on which to arrange your marriage certificates and the register. A card table is a good size.

During the ceremony itself *look at* the celebrant or reader. Try not to be distracted by anyone's movements or comments or to get edgy: stand straight and relaxed — fidgeting, slouching, putting your hands in your pockets, or staring around the sky, is sure to put off a celebrant, and everyone else.

When you take your vows, it is a special moment between you and your partner. In a sense, it is a moment when you should forget everyone else, including the celebrant. When repeating your vows you should look at your partner. I feel that sometimes people miss one of the best moments of their lives when, through shyness or embarrassment, they do not make the moment of the vows their own.

A practical hint: rings will slide on more easily if before the ceremony you rub a little Vaseline or soap inside the ring.

If little children or babies are at a ceremony, it is best to ask the mothers to sit or stand near the door so that they can take the children out if necessary.

ORCHESTRATING THE CEREMONY: THE CELEBRANT'S ROLE

The first thing I wish to do here is to pass on some advice (learnt by many mistakes) to celebrants. A successful wedding means attention (albeit instinctive) to a great number of details.

The basic principle is that the ceremony must be *heard*; only then, as the old dictum says, can it be *understood* and *appreciated*. This means that you must gather all the company together, close enough to hear you and the couple. People hang back, but if they are asked to come closer to create 'a proper atmosphere' I always find they co-operate.

Before the ceremony, brief the groom and bride to look at you during the ceremony, and to look at each other during the vows and the giving of rings — and, of course, when they are invited to kiss each other!

Having tried all sorts of arrangements, I feel that the best arrangement for most marriages is a circle or semi-circle of the bridal party and guests.

The celebrant should take up a suitable position to address the guests and/or the couple. Giving attention to the assembled company in the introductory remarks makes everyone interested and involved.

Usually, if there is a person giving away or presenting the bride, I place that person between the bride and groom. This seems to me to preserve the symbolism of the bride being part of her family until the vows that constitute the marriage are completed. Once the question is asked, that person joins the other guests. If both parents of the bride and groom give their son and daughter away, then I place them at the edges of the bridal party.

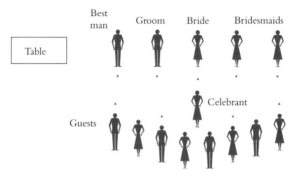

Photographs are important for most people. In suggesting a place for the bridal party to stand, consider the background carefully. Avoid mirrors. Curtains, candles, flowers and pictures often provide a good background indoors, while out of doors it is a matter of choosing the best trees and flowers.

Any celebrant who feels that the guests are not settled should ask very seriously to be given absolute attention during the ceremony. It seems trite to say, but it is important for the celebrant to speak with sincerity. Do not stand too close to the couple (for the sake of their eardrums), and only move closer when reminding them of movement, such as to turn and face each other during the vows, and to indicate which finger to put the ring on, or to give each other the traditional kiss once they have been declared husband and wife.

In the usual pattern of ceremony the celebrant is called on to play a prominent role. It does not, however, have to be like this. By law the celebrant does not have to say a word or do anything; it is sufficient if the parties say their vows in the celebrant's presence. I have been the official celebrant at marriages where no one knew I was there until the signing (even then it is possible to stay out of the way!).

The couple marry each other. They can arrange the whole marriage themselves and/or with the participation of friends. A string of people can sing songs, recite poetry, say a few words, play a favourite record or tape, and so on. The best atmosphere is created when everyone sings together.

A Personally-composed Wedding Ceremony

Every wedding ceremony should have some basic structure. For example:
- chosen music or song
- a welcome to those attending
- an introduction that explains the views of the couple, their values, their ideals, their hopes for the relationship. It may express the hope that their marriage has good effects for their own family, their friends and the wider community of the world (with quotations, where and if applicable)
- a reading, or readings
- in Australia, a Monitum from the Marriage Act
- the giving away or presentation of the bride (optional)
- the marriage commitment, which traditionally consists of the asking/question and the vows
- the giving of a ring or exchange of rings
- another reading or readings (optional)
- declaration of the marriage — a statement that a marriage sealed by a wedding has taken place
- the signing of the register and certificates, during which special music is played (live or from CDs) or songs are sung (soloists, choir, or all together!)
- the presentation of the certificate by the celebrant to the couple
- recessional song or music.

If you have a mind to be really personal, take up your pen, or lean forward to your computer, and analyse and articulate your own thoughts and feelings. Dig deep into the loves of your own literary and musical experience.

When you are composing a personal introduction, the following questions may help:

How did you first meet?

When did you first fall in love?

When did you decide you wanted to be with one another for ever?

What were the good things that helped you decide?

What were the difficulties?

What do you (groom) like/love about her?

What do you (bride) like/love about him?

Why did you decide to have a ceremony?

What special reason did you have for deciding on the place for the ceremony?

What does your family mean to you?

What do your friends mean to you?

What are your hopes for the future?

Expressing yourself well is no easy task. There is nothing wrong with getting the help of friends. It is wise to consult the celebrant at the end of your first draft — at least for checking the structure. Some celebrants are very good at assisting in writing a personalised wedding, but this should not be expected as part of the task.

It is a great help if you neatly present your ceremony on small pages so that the celebrant does not have large unwieldy pages from which to read at the actual ceremony.

MUSIC

Music is integral to most ceremonies, and should be planned as part of the wedding ceremony. Many people prefer live music, and it is an ideal of celebrant ceremonies to develop the arts, and to give opportunities for our musicians, poets and other artists to become more a part of our mainstream ceremonial culture.

It is also appropriate for you to have the music that has

significance for you, as live music, or on CDs and tapes — CDs are much easier to work with.

When is the wedding music played?

- As background music while waiting for the ceremony to start (say, 15 minutes). This music should stop when word comes that the bride is near! (Note that background music during the words of the ceremony rarely works; avoid this if possible.)
- As a processional: specially chosen music should be played for the entrance of the bride (2–3 minutes).
- During the signing: this is the best opportunity for special music and song (7–8 minutes when you allow for photographs).
- During the recessional: play special music or song immediately the celebrant presents the couple with the *Certificate of Marriage*.
- After the ceremony while congratulations are being given and drinks are being served.

What sort of performers should you choose?

- Musicians: quartets, trios, jazz groups, violinists, pipers, harpists, piano accordionists, keyboarders, etc. Ensure that you hire talented and co-operative people. It is important that the musicians are placed as close to the wedding party as practicable (not under a tree a long way away).
- Singers: sopranos, pop singers, barbershop quartets, and choirs.
- Singing together: nothing beats this! Everyone must have a copy of the words of the songs; it must be played in a key most people can cope with, and it must be led by a competent singer or singers. (See the end of the book of a list of suggested songs.)

CHOICE OF VENUE

The media always love to report 'gimmicky' marriages (those on top of a mountain in winter, under water, while skydiving, on the back of motorbikes, etc.), but such weddings are extremely rare. All celebrants will testify that marriages celebrated in gimmicky places are very serious commitments just the same. In a way it is a testimony to the belief of the couple that their love and their union is unique, and the place usually has some sentimental value.

Marriages on a beach or in a park garden, have traps for planners. There should be an alternative place close by in case of rain or wind. On the day, where there is any doubt, the best plan is for the celebrant and guests to meet at the main place decided on, look at the sky, make a decision, then if necessary proceed in convoy to the alternative venue. Instructions like 'If it is raining, go instead to 37 Smith Street' never work, as half the guests will end up at the park and the other half at Smith Street.

Choosing parks and gardens can have other pitfalls. Avoid proximity to traffic intersections — the noise can drown out the words and make the whole event close to meaningless. Also avoid pathways full of staring, talking strangers, and especially youngsters doing wheelies on bikes or on skateboards. In all garden weddings where I sense such dangers, I usually ask one of the groomsmen or a capable guest to ask the youngsters to play or ride their bikes away from the scene.

READINGS

If you are a reader at a marriage you may be nervous. Your reading will not be successful if you give way to nervous haste. Practise your reading beforehand, read slowly and clearly, and look at your audience from time to time. Ceremonial reading is much slower than broadcasting or lecturing, and will lose force if it is rushed.

Readers should be part of the rehearsal, and should practise their readings in full at that time.

Type of Wedding Ceremonies

The next chapter gives examples of actual wedding ceremonies. From time immemorial it has always been the prerogative of the people who are marrying (through their culture and their families), to express their commitment in their own way. It is only in recent times that the church and/or the state has been involved in witnessing marriage. Clergymen and civil celebrants are witnesses only.

It is one of the strange paradoxes of life that both church and state seem to have 'taken over' the marriage ceremony. It is not the celebrant who 'marries' them. Celebrants feel privileged to be official witnesses, and are anxious to see people's rights restored in the marriage ceremony. Informed celebrants believe that couples should have the sort of marriage they want, where they want, and when they want it.

Despite what may seem to be implied in the following pages, you should feel free to write your own ceremony, to alter any wording, or include any material you feel is appropriate for you. The celebrant, as a witness to the basic contract of marriage, is anxious to oblige you.

We always surround important occasions with ceremony and celebration, but it has to be just right. People get upset if the ceremony is too short or too long.

Much depends on the style of the people involved. In the following pages you should find something to suit you, or at least to get you started.

The first ceremony (a longer one), for *Romeo* and *Juliet*, is one I was asked to write for a magazine. I am convinced that Australian/Western culture is broadening, and people of discernment now want more music and poetry than they did ten or fifteen years ago.

Most people wish wedding ceremonies to be dignified, simple and not too long. There is no fear of this in the next four ceremonies, as they are (except for the first one) of the recommended minimum length. I have included a selection of readings, and a number of alternatives.

For convenience, each ceremony is divided into sections. I have decided on this method so that you will find it easier to set out a well-planned ceremony and/or replace sections with material from elsewhere, or with what you have written yourselves.

Chapters 2 and 3 give you the content of the wedding

ceremony; chapter 4 has further information on traditions and symbols.

The Australian Federation of Civil Celebrants sets the following standard of service for a quality wedding ceremony:

- You are supplied with a copy of *Ceremonies & Celebrations*, or an equivalent.
- You are given complete choice of your ceremony.
- At a relaxed interview with the celebrant you can discuss all your wedding requirements.
- You are entitled to unlimited consultation by phone or in person with the celebrant.
- You are entitled to a rehearsal at the celebrant's office or an on-site rehearsal (within a reasonable distance).
- The production of a printed copy of your ceremony (if you do not wish to do this yourselves).
- Your wedding certificate is prepared in calligraphy, or laser printing.
- Appreciation certificates are provided for the bridal party and others on request.
- Ample time — a guarantee that no other wedding will be booked so close that the celebrant arrives late or rushes out in an unseemly manner.
- A personal guarantee that the celebrant will become familiar with the ceremony beforehand, and will speak in a sincere and interested manner.
- As far as possible, the celebrant will dress to fit in with your wedding (a male celebrant, for example, could wear a lounge suit, a lounge suit with an academic gown, or a dinner suit, as appropriate; a female celebrant should dress to suit the formality or informality of the ceremony).

Wedding Checklist

BEFORE THE WEDDING

Check that you have organised the following:
- a celebrant, and the ceremony (including the music)
- the wedding ring/s

- the venue for the ceremony (and an alternative, if necessary)
- the bridesmaid/s and groomsman/men
- the wedding dress and suit
- the flowers for the bridal party, and for the venue
- the photographer
- the place for the reception, the caterers, the menu and drinks
- the wedding cake
- the invitations, place cards, and thank-you notes
- appointments with the hairdresser
- the arrangements for the honeymoon.

AFTER THE WEDDING

Check that you have arranged the following:
- address and name change (if applicable) for driver's licence, passport, insurance, accounts, etc.
- make or revise your wills
- sent thank-you notes.

TOASTS AND SPEECHES AT THE RECEPTION

It is traditional to have the following toasts and speeches:
- the toast to the bride and groom, proposed by a person chosen in advance by the couple
- the reply by the groom, and/or bride.

(Some choose to end the toasts and speeches at this point.)
At the conclusion of this response:
- the groom proposes a toast to the bridesmaids
- the best man/bridesmaid replies, and reads any messages.

(At some receptions the toasts and speeches end here.)

Other optional toasts and speeches are:
- to the parents of the bride
- the father or mother of the bride replies
- to the parents of the groom
- the father or mother of the groom replies.

This arrangement varies frequently. It is completely accept-able for a bride, bridesmaid or mother to reply to, or propose, toasts.

THE CUTTING OF THE CAKE

The speeches, toasts, and the cutting of the cake can take place at any time. Usually they occur at any time during the refresh-ments after the wedding ceremony at an informal ceremony, or after the main course at a formal wedding breakfast.

2 The Wedding Ceremony

Ceremony 1: *Romeo** and *Juliet**
(10–12 minutes)

I wrote this ceremony (my favourite wedding ceremony), on request, for a wedding magazine.

> *The wedding ceremony for Romeo Dante Knightley and Juliet Beatrice Woodhouse takes place at Queen's Hall, Parliament House, Melbourne, Victoria*

The Perfect Fourth String Quartet plays background music as the guests arrive and take their seats, which are arranged in an intimate semi-circle, the first row of which starts about 3 metres from the wedding party so as not to lose intimacy and atmosphere. There is a red carpet and aisle in the centre of the semi-circle through which the bridal procession enters. The groom and groomsmen are in place.

As the bride reaches the top steps, to begin her entrance

---

*In this and all other ceremonies, substitute your own names and the names of the other people involved for the names in italics.

through the front door of Parliament House and process through the foyer, Placido Domingo and Maureen McGovern sing 'A Love Until the End of Time' (if you can't book Placido and Maureen or singers of their class, a CD will suffice!). Top-quality speakers are arranged behind the wedding party, possibly obscured by flowers or decorations so that the sound is still excellent and the aesthetics pleasing.

When the wedding party is in place the celebrant (having already ensured that all the guests are also in place) begins.

INTRODUCTION [WI 1]

Celebrant: The great medieval philosopher, Thomas Aquinas, when asked to define true love, said that it was 'to will the good of the other person'. If you truly love someone you want their success, their happiness, everything that is best for them. In the history of the world great lovers have died for the one or the ones they love.

Nothing like that is called for here, but *Romeo* and *Juliet* do want you to know why they are marrying today. They could have chosen simply to live together. This seemingly is a 'safer' course, would give them more options, sustain their freedom, with fewer risks. They have thought about this, and have decided that for them it is not enough.

They see this ceremony today as a stronger commitment to their relationship. They call you together, their friends and family, to make this commitment clear to you and to call on your acknowledgement and support. They publicly call on each other to take the relationship much more seriously.

Juliet and *Romeo* recognise that they are very happy with one another. They recognise that they would not be happier with anyone else — that no distant fields are greener.

There is another element in all this. They love each other. With the philosopher, they *will* each other's good. They *will* each other's success, fulfilment and happiness.

They know the main danger in a marriage relationship is the danger of taking each other for granted, of not appreciating each other enough. So they want to stay aware of each other. They know they must communicate with each other and be open to communication. This, they know, is a lot harder than it sounds. Words must be said softly, listened to carefully.

Their relationship must be sustained by the will to express it — the loving word, the loving smile, the loving embrace, the loving favour, the giving with graciousness and generosity. They know not to take without giving, give without taking. A true lover knows what the demands of love sometimes cost the partner — so they *will* to be sensitive, to be appreciative. And they remind themselves today that they must do these things without dominating, without smothering, without suffocating the other.

They have assessed happily that their relationship is for life. They have found each other, they like each other, they love each other, they want it to last, they intend it to last, they will it to last.

More than that, they will it to get better, they will it to get deeper. They want to be husband and wife. They want people to look at them and quote, as it were, the poet Homer, who said, 800 years before Christ: 'There is nothing nobler or more admirable than when two people who see eye to eye keep house as man and wife, confounding their enemies and delighting their friends'.

READINGS

It is important that readers have a strong voice or a microphone so that they can be heard by everyone. All readers should be aware that ceremonial reading is much slower than other reading. *Siobhan* should stand in the middle of the aisle and address the bride and groom.

The celebrant usually introduces each reader by name.

Siobhan: *Juliet*, *Romeo*,
To deepen your reflections on love and marriage you have chosen the profound and famous words of William Shakespeare:

Sonnet 116 [WR 1]

Let me not to the marriage of true minds
Admit impediments. Love is not love
Which alters when it alteration finds,
Or bends with the remover to remove:
O, no! it is an ever-fixed mark,
That looks on tempests and is never shaken;
It is the star to every wandering bark,
Whose worth's unknown, although his height be taken.
Love's not Time's fool, though rosy lips and cheeks
Within his bending sickle's compass come;
Love alters not with his brief hours and weeks,
But bears it out even to the edge of doom.
If this be error and upon me proved,
I never writ, nor no man ever loved.

Justin: *Romeo* and *Juliet*,
D. H. Lawrence wrote of the deep strength of a relationship
that comes from true love:

The Gem [WR 2]

And man and woman are like the earth,
that brings forth flowers in Summer, and love,
but underneath is rock.
Older than flowers, older than ferns,
    older than foraminiferae,
older than plasm altogether is the soul of man
    underneath;
and when, throughout all the wild orgasms of love,
slowly a gem forms, in the ancient, once-more-molten
    rocks of two human hearts, two ancient rocks,
a man's heart and a woman's,
that is the crystal of peace, the slow hard jewel of trust,
the gem of mutual peace emerging from the wild chaos
    of love.

MONITUM FROM THE MARRIAGE ACT [M 1]

Read by the celebrant, this is a solemn warning about marriage, adapted from the Marriage Act:

> Now I, *Dulcie Citizen*, a civil celebrant,
> am duly authorised by the law
> to solemnise this, your marriage,
> according to the laws of Australia.
>
> Before you, *Romeo*, and you, *Juliet*,
> are joined together in marriage in my presence
> and in the presence of these, your family and friends,
> I am bound, as you know, to remind you publicly
> of the solemn, the serious and the binding nature
> of the relationship into which you are now about
>   to enter.
>
> Marriage, as most of us understand it,
> is the voluntary and full commitment
> of a man to a woman,
> and a woman to a man.
> It is made in the deepest sense
> to the exclusion of all others,
> and is entered into with the desire,
> the hope and the firm intention
> that it will last for life.

Celebrants are generally required by law to read this, or words to this effect, although some are exempt.

GIVING AWAY/PRESENTATION OF THE BRIDE
[GA 1]

Celebrant: When thinking people conclude what are the real values in life, and come to decide what really matters, they always come back to one value — human relationships.

One of the most understated but deepest relationships in human life is that between the caring father and the loving daughter. One of the rare occasions this relationship is acknowledged is at a wedding ceremony. *Brian* represents all of us, he particularly represents his family, but today in a special gesture he symbolises his own personal love for his daughter.

(The celebrant turns to the father of the bride or the person giving the bride away.) So, mindful of these values, I now ask him, 'Who presents this woman to be married to this man?'

Brian: I do.

He then gestures towards his daughter, and immediately joins the other guests.

THE ASKING [A 1]

Celebrant to the groom: *Romeo,*
 Will you take *Juliet* to be your lawful wedded wife?
 Will you love and respect her,
 be honest with her,
 and stand by her through whatever may come,
 so you can genuinely share your life together?

Groom: I will.

Celebrant to the bride: *Juliet,*
 Will you take *Romeo* to be your lawful wedded husband?
 Will you love and respect him,
 be honest with him,
 and stand by him through whatever may come,
 so you can genuinely share your life together?

Bride: I will.

VOWS [WV 1]

The celebrant quietly asks the couple to face each other and look at each other, to hold both hands, and to repeat the vows, phrase by phrase, after the celebrant.

Groom:
 I, *Romeo*, take you, *Juliet*, as my wife.
 I pledge to share my life openly with you,
 to speak the truth to you in love.

I promise to honour and tenderly care for you,
to cherish and encourage your own fulfilment as an
    individual,
for the rest of my life.

Bride:
I, *Juliet*, take you, *Romeo*, as my husband.
I pledge to share my life openly with you,
to speak the truth to you in love.
I promise to honour and tenderly care for you,
to cherish and encourage your own fulfilment as an
    individual,
for the rest of my life.

RING CEREMONY [RC 1]

The couple stay in the same position.

The celebrant takes the bride's ring from the best man and gives it to the groom, who holds it over the tip of the appropriate finger, and repeats the words, phrase by phrase, after the celebrant.

The groom then slides the ring onto the bride's finger.

If there are rings for both, this procedure is repeated by the bride.

Groom: *Juliet,*
This ring I give you,
it is my personal gift,
my personal promise of love and trust,
and pride that you are my wife.

Bride: *Romeo,*
This ring I give you,
it is my personal gift,
my personal promise of love and trust,
and pride that you are my husband.

READINGS

Main bridesmaid: This reading you have chosen reminds us that this day will be special for you forever.

Come Take My Hand [WR 3]

Come take my hand
And walk with me
Into the future
As was planned.

For every year upon this day,
Your eyes shall meet
Above the toasting glass,
And you shall pledge again
With outstretched hands.

Best man: This reading is by Sir Philip Sidney:

The Bargain [WR 4]

My true love hath my heart, and I have his,
By just exchange one for another given:
I hold his dear, and mine he cannot miss,
There never was a better bargain driven:
His heart in me keeps him and me in one,
My heart in him his thoughts and senses guides:
He loves my heart, for once it was his own,
I cherish his, because in me it bides:

My true love hath my heart, and I have his.

Other bridesmaid: This reading you have chosen is to express the knowledge you have that you are friends as well as lovers. I will read these words as you would read them to each other.

Today [WR 5]

Today I marry my friend,
The one I have laughed with and cried with,
the one I have learned from and shared with,
the one I have chosen to support,
encourage and give myself to,
through all the days given us to share.

Today I marry the one I love.

Groomsman:

Love Is the Reason [WR 6]

Love is the reason why this day
Was chosen by you both
To begin your lives together —

And love is the reason why you both
Will give with all your hearts
For the good of each other.

Love is the reason
That together you will become one —
One in hope,
One in believing in life, and
One in sharing the coming years.

Celebrant: This famous and beautiful poem is by Christopher Brennan:

Because She Would Ask Me Why I Loved Her
[WR 7]

If questioning would make us wise
No eyes would ever gaze in eyes;
If all our tale were told in speech
No mouths would wander each to each.

Were spirits free from mortal mesh
And love not bound in hearts of flesh
No aching breasts would yearn to meet
And find their ecstasy complete.

For who is there that lives and knows
The secret powers by which he grows?
Were knowledge all, what were our need
To thrill and faint and sweetly bleed?

Then seek not, sweet, the 'If' and 'Why'
I love you now until I die:
For I must love because I live
And life in me is what you give.

Groom's mother: *Juliet*, *Romeo*,
We finish these thoughts with a wish for you.

The Apache Wedding Prayer [WR 8]

Now you will feel no rain,
for each will be shelter for the other.

Now you will feel no cold,
for each will be warmth for the other

Now you will feel no loneliness,
for each of you will be companion to the other.

Now you are two persons,
but there are three lives before you:
his life, her life, and your life together.

May beauty surround you both
on the journey ahead and through all the years.

May happiness be your companion
to the place where the river meets the sun.

Go now to your dwelling
to enter into the days of your life together.

And may your days be good
And long upon the earth.

Traditional

DECLARATION OF MARRIAGE [DM 1]

Celebrant: Ladies and Gentlemen,
Romeo and *Juliet* have declared before all of us that they will
live together in marriage. They have made special promises to
each other. They have symbolised it by joining hands, taking
vows, and by exchanging rings.

So, therefore, on your behalf and on behalf of the community, I now declare *Romeo* and *Juliet* to be husband and wife.

The bride and groom kiss.

THE SIGNING

During the signing of the register and the marriage certifi-
cate, musicians or singers perform or a recording is played of
Anthony Warlow and Marina Prior singing 'Love Me, That's
All I Ask of You' from *The Phantom of the Opera*; followed by
Nat King Cole's song 'When I Fall in Love It Will Be Forever'.

The celebrant presents the couple (properly the bride,
according to tradition) with their marriage certificate.

During the ensuing congratulations the Perfect Fourth
String Quartet plays beautiful background music.

This concludes the ceremony, and all the proceedings as
far as the celebrant is concerned.

Ceremony 2: *Mary* and *John*
(5–7 minutes)

INTRODUCTION [WI 2]

Celebrant: Friends,
I call upon everyone here present to be a fellow-witness with
me in this union between *John* and *Mary*. We are here, not only
to witness their commitment to each other, but also to wish
them well and every happiness for their life together.

Mary and *John* believe this union is founded on that sort
of sincerity and understanding that leads to tolerance, confidence and trust. They feel it involves respect for each other's
individuality, and a difficult task, the acceptance of each
other's weaknesses, prejudices and faults. They believe too
that those qualities that have attracted each to the other can
obviously be best developed during a life spent together.

We are here because *John* and *Mary* do not, and cannot,
live in isolation. The experience of their love touches all of us,
and it is fitting that we should celebrate their happiness. This
ceremony gives public recognition to the private experience
of their love. At a different level we share in it, we rejoice for
them, and we support them.

A happy union, they know, will enable them to establish a

home where there will be love and stability, where you, their family and their friends, will find welcome, peace and support, and which will be a base from which the influence of their shared lives, and we hope lives strengthened today by this ceremony, can extend.

(Or use any of the alternative introductions, or write your own based on these introductions and from elsewhere.)

READING

Celebrant or a reader to the couple: *John* and *Mary*, The reading you have chosen has been inspired by Walter Rinder's *Love Is an Attitude* (or use one of the alternative readings).

Learn How to Love [WR 9]

Every day you live,
Learn how to love.

Take time with each other,
Restore each other's soul with loving words.

Receive love with as much understanding
As you give it.

Find that which is within yourselves
Then you can share it with each other.

Do not fear this love,
And do not fear this marriage,
But keep open hearts and sincere minds.

Be sincerely interested in each other's happiness;
Be, too, constant and consistent in your love,
And in your actions.

From this, as you know, comes security and strength.
All that we love deeply becomes a part of us,
So, even though you retain your individuality,
Today in a real sense you also become one
In a true unity.

That this may be deep and rewarding,
Today, the day of your marriage,
Try to commit yourselves,
Fully and freely and trustingly,
To each other, without reservations.

MONITUM FROM THE MARRIAGE ACT

[M1, see Ceremony 1]

GIVING AWAY/PRESENTATION OF THE BRIDE

(optional) [GA 2]

Celebrant (turning to the father of the bride or the person giving the bride away): Who presents this woman to be married to this man?

Father/other person: I do.

This person gestures towards the bride, then joins the other guests.

(Or use any of the other Giving Away/Presentation ceremonies; there is one involving both parents.)

THE ASKING (optional) [A 2]

Celebrant to the groom: *John*,
Will you take *Mary* to be your lawful wife?
Will you love her, comfort her,
honour and keep her, in sickness and in health,
and, forsaking all others, keep only unto her,
so long as you both shall live?

Groom: I will.

Celebrant to the bride: *Mary*,
Will you take *John* to be your lawful husband?
Will you love him, comfort him,
honour and keep him, in sickness and in health,
and, forsaking all others, keep only unto him,
so long as you both shall live?

Bride: I will.

(Or use any of the other Askings.)

VOWS [WV 2]

The vows are the basic legal substructure of the marriage ceremony. The asking must always be followed by a definite statement of vows.

The celebrant quietly asks the couple to face each other and look at each other, to hold both hands, and to repeat the vows, phrase by phrase, after the celebrant.

Groom:
I, *John*, take you, *Mary*, to be my lawful wife,
to have and to hold, from this day forward,
for better for worse, for richer for poorer,
in sickness and in health,
to love and to cherish,
for the rest of my life.

Bride:
I, *Mary*, take you, *John*,
to be my lawful husband,
to have and to hold, from this day forward,
for better for worse, for richer for poorer,
in sickness and in health,
to love and to cherish,
for the rest of my life.

(Or use any of the other Vows.)

RING CEREMONY [RC 2]

(See Ceremony 1 for the procedure here.)

Groom: *Mary*,
With this ring,
I thee wed.
Take and wear it as a pledge of my love,
and as a symbol of all we share.

READINGS

(Celebrant/or reader): The next reading you have chosen is a simple poem.

Now We Are One [WR 10]

When thoughts take wing
a wedding ring encircles all our dreams,
and love abounds above, around,
enriching all our schemes.

We plan together all our life
to make our dreams come true,
when love is there a smile, a prayer,
a hug, a kiss, will do.

And then together, hand in hand,
we go with love we've won,
and you will see the you and me
that once were two — are one.

Kate Fisher

(Or use any of the other readings)

Celebrant, immediately after the last ring has been placed:

Sharing [WR 11]

There is no greater happiness than that of sharing life,
With all its joys, and all its cares, as a loving husband and
wife.
For love gives life new meaning, and has a special way
Of growing stronger, and deeper, with every passing day.
Yes, life is so much happier and brighter when you're
sharing
The very special joys that come with loving and giving
and caring.

(Or use any of the Other Ring Ceremonies.)

DECLARATION OF MARRIAGE [DM 2]

Celebrant to the guests: Ladies and Gentlemen,
John and *Mary* have declared before all of us that they will live together in marriage. They have made special promises to each other. They have symbolised it by joining hands, taking vows, and by giving a ring (*or* by exchanging rings).

So, therefore, on your behalf and on behalf of the community, I now declare them to be husband and wife.

The bride and groom kiss.

THE SIGNING

The register and the marriage certificate are signed. The celebrant presents the couple (properly the bride, according to tradition) with their certificate.

This concludes the ceremony, and all the proceedings for the celebrant.

Ceremony 3: Todd and Jane

INTRODUCTION [WI 3]

Celebrant to the guests: Friends, welcome!
Real love in marriage is something beyond the warmth and glow, the excitement and romance, of being deeply in love. It is caring as much about the welfare and happiness of your marriage partner as about your own. But real love is not being totally absorbed in each other. It means looking outward in the same direction, together.

Love makes burdens lighter because you divide them, it makes joys more intense because you share them. It makes you stronger so you can reach out and become involved with life in ways you would never dare risk alone.

The beautiful thing about love is that it is an experience we share with all people throughout the world. Yet to everyone who falls in love it is the most unique and precious thing in the world.

A really happy marriage is founded on love. Love is, of its nature, unselfish, understanding and kind. True love, too, is a commitment of heart and a commitment of mind. There can be no stronger bond to ensure and secure a happy married life.

Harmonious wedded life is a precious gain to both a man and a woman because, even though marriage increases the scope of responsibility, it does add that dimension of love to life, giving it new meaning and purpose.

Celebrant to the couple: On this day, *Todd* and *Jane*, the day of your marriage, you are standing somewhat apart from the rest of us as a symbol of the open expression of your love. And this is as it should be, but love is not meant to be the possession of two people alone. Rather it should be the source of a common energy, an energy that gives you the strength to live your lives with joy and courage.

READING

Celebrant (or reader): *Todd* and *Jane*,
The reading you have chosen is by the poet Gloria Matthew:

Marriage Is Love [WR12]

If two are caring, as they're sharing life's hopes and fears,
If the music of laughter outweighs the sadness of tears,
Marriage is togetherness.

If both derive pleasure from mere presence of each
    other,
Yet no jealousies restrict, worry or smother,
Marriage is freedom.

If achievements mean more when they benefit two,
And consideration is shown with each point of view,
Marriage is respect.

And if togetherness, freedom and respect are combined
With a joy that words can never fully define,
Then marriage is love.

(Or use any of the alternative introductions, or write your own based on these introductions and from elsewhere.)

MONITUM FROM THE MARRIAGE ACT

[M1, see Ceremony 1]

GIVING AWAY/PRESENTATION OF THE BRIDE

(optional) [GA 3]

Celebrant: These are the days of equality but, as you know, in ancient times it was the custom for a young woman to be under the authority and protection of the man who was the head of her household — usually her father or elder brother. When she married, the responsibility — and the authority — passed to her husband. This was the origin of the Giving Away ceremony.

Times have changed, men and women have changed, but we still remember this as an ancient custom. These days we like to make it the occasion when the families and friends of the bride and groom show their approval of the marriage. Since you are all here, we may take it that this is token enough, and invite *Max* to speak on behalf of all present.

(The celebrant turns to the father or the person giving the bride away.) Who, then, on behalf of all of us, presents this woman to be married to this man?

Max: I do.

He indicates the bride, then joins the other guests.

(Or use any of the other Giving Away/Presentation ceremonies; there is one involving both parents.)

THE ASKING (optional) [A 3]

Celebrant to the groom:

Will you, *Todd*, take *Jane* to be your lifelong spouse?

Will you make the daily effort to relate to her and listen to her?

Will you be gracious and generous in your giving of yourself?

Will you work for what is best for her for the rest of your life?

Groom: I will.

Celebrant to the bride:

> Will you, *Jane*, take *Todd* to be your lifelong spouse?
> Will you make the daily effort to relate to her and listen to her?
> Will you be gracious and generous in your giving of yourself?
> Will you work for what is best for her for the rest of your life?

Bride: I will.

(Or use any of the other Askings.)

VOWS [WV 3]

The vows are the basic legal substructure of the marriage ceremony. The asking must always be followed by a definite statement of vows.

The celebrant quietly asks the couple to face each other and look at each other, to hold both hands, and to repeat the vows, phrase by phrase, after the celebrant.

Groom:

> I, *Todd*, take you, *Jane*, to be my lawful wife.
> I will try to be a loving husband.
> I promise to respect you as an individual.
> I intend to develop as a person in partnership with you.
> I want to love you through good fortune and adversity, while we both shall live.

Bride:

> I, *Jane*, take you, *Todd*, to be my lawful husband.
> I will try to be a loving wife.
> I promise to respect you as an individual.
> I intend to develop as a person in partnership with you.
> I want to love you through good fortune and adversity, while we both shall live.

(Or use any of the other Vows.)

RING CEREMONY [RC 3]

(See Ceremony 1 for the procedure here.)

Groom:

> *Jane*, with this ring,
> I wed you,
> and pledge my faithful love.

(Or use any of the other Ring Ceremonies.)

READINGS

Celebrant, as the last ring is being placed:

> **Endlessness** [WR 13]
>
> The roundness of your ring
> betokens the endlessness of love,
> its pure metal speaks of the purity of love,
> its value reminds you that you should defend and protect
> that which you hold most valuable in life.
> Wear it with love and honour.

(This reading is easily adapted for two rings.)

Celebrant (or reader) to the couple: *Todd* and *Jane*, the next reading you have chosen is a poem:

> **We Will Not Wish You Joy** [WR 14]
>
> We will not wish you joy on this great day,
> For joy is in your hearts and goes with you
> Along the fragrant, mystic, sunlit way;
> We will not wish you joy whilst love is new.
>
> But this is our wish: May you be strong enough
> To shelter love, and keep it safe from harm,
> When winds blow high, and roads are steep and rough,
> May you protect your love, preserve its charm.

When days are dark, may love be your sure light
When days are cold, may love be your bright fire,
Your guiding star when Hope is out of sight,
The essence and the sum of your desire.

May love be with you through the flight of years,
Then after storms, there always will be calm.
Though you have cause for heartache and for tears,
Despair lasts not, where love is there for balm.

This be the prayer we breathe for you today:
When you have reached the summit of Life's hill,
May it be possible for you to say,
'Married long years, but we are lovers still'.

(Or use any of the other readings.)

DECLARATION OF MARRIAGE [DM 3]

Celebrant to the guests: Ladies and Gentlemen,
Todd and *Jane* have declared before all of us that they will live
together in marriage. They have made special promises to
each other. They have symbolised it by joining hands, taking
vows, and by giving a ring (*or* by exchanging rings).

So, therefore, on your behalf and on behalf of the community, I now declare them to be husband and wife.

The bride and groom kiss.

THE SIGNING

The register and the marriage certificate are signed. The celebrant presents the couple (properly the bride, according to
tradition) with their certificate.

This concludes the ceremony, and all the proceedings as
far as the celebrant is concerned.

Ceremony 4: *Linda* and *David*

INTRODUCTION [WI 4]

Celebrant to the guests: A warm welcome to all!

Every wedding ceremony at which a clergyman, a rabbi or a celebrant, like myself, officiates is, of course, of a marriage that already exists. This ceremony gives social recognition to a union that has already taken place in the hearts of this couple.

It is *David*'s and *Linda*'s wish at this time to declare their marriage partnership to the world. It is a statement of commitment to each other and to the ideals they already have.

In their belief their union is based not only on mutual love but on the desire to work together for the development of a union of spirit, for their own personal fulfilment, and for the attainment of mutual goals and ambitions.

Together they hope to discover truth in life. They intend to encourage each other to act according to what is best for their world, their children and themselves.

Linda and *David* recognise not only the need for loving commitment to each other but also to humane principles of living and to the best of human values.

READING

Celebrant (or reader): *Linda* and *David*,

The reading you have chosen is by the poet Gloria Matthew:

Marriage Lines [WR 15]

In a marriage where love lives
There's realism and truth,
There's pleasure in giving of time.
Closeness and security,
Freedom for individuality,
No need to possess or confine.

In a marriage where love lives
True friendship is present
With respect for each point of view.

Through disappointment sharing
Comes deeper caring
Happiness deeper for two.

In a marriage where love lives
There's no need for rules,
There's understanding if harsh words are spoken.
Apologies are accepted,
Trust is effected,
The true bonds of love never broken.

(Or use any of the alternative introductions, or write your own based on these introductions and from elsewhere.)

MONITUM FROM THE MARRIAGE ACT

[M 1, see Ceremony 1]

GIVING AWAY/PRESENTATION OF THE BRIDE

(optional) [GA 4]

Celebrant (turning to the father of the bride or the person giving the bride away): Who presents this woman to be married to this man?

Father (or other person): I do.

He indicates the bride, then joins the other guests.

(Or use any of the other Giving Away ceremonies; there is one involving both parents.)

THE ASKING [A 4]

Celebrant to the groom:
David, will you take *Linda* to be your wife, your lifelong partner?
Will you constantly try to stay aware of your relationship with her, striving to communicate with her, sensitive to her needs, wanting her success and happiness through all the years ahead?

Groom: I will.

Celebrant to the bride:

> *Linda*, will you take *David* to be your husband, your life-long partner?
>
> Will you constantly try to stay aware of your relationship with him, striving to communicate with him, sensitive to his needs, wanting his success and happiness through all the years ahead?

Bride: I will.

(Or use any of the other Askings.)

VOWS   [WV 4]

The vows are the basic legal substructure of the marriage ceremony. The asking must always be followed by a definite statement of vows.

The celebrant quietly asks the couple to face each other and look at each other, to hold both hands, and to repeat the vows, phrase by phrase, after the celebrant.

Groom:

> I, *David*, take you, *Linda*, as my wife.
>
> I pledge to share my life openly with you,
>
> to speak the truth to you in love.
>
> I promise to honour and tenderly care for you,
>
> to cherish and encourage your own fulfilment as an individual,
>
> for the rest of my life.

Bride:

> I, *Linda*, take you, *David*, as my husband.
>
> I pledge to share my life openly with you,
>
> to speak the truth to you in love.
>
> I promise to honour and tenderly care for you,
>
> to cherish and encourage your own fulfilment as an individual,
>
> for the rest of my life.

(Or use any of the other Vows.)

RING CEREMONY [RC 4]

(See Ceremony 1 for the procedure here.)

Groom: *Linda,*
> This ring means that I give myself to you,
> a seal of my unending love.

(Or use any of the other Ring Ceremonies.)

READINGS

Celebrant, as the last ring is being placed:

The Depth of Love [WR16]

Had I not known the depth of love
Life would have been the poorer —
But with the happiness it brings
Nothing could be surer.

For love is — just relaxing,
And trusting, and believing,
Just the very simple process
Of giving and receiving.

(Or use any of the other readings.)

Celebrant (or reader): *David* and *Linda*, the final reading you have chosen is by the poet Rod McKuen:

Taking Time to Love [WR17]

Taking time to love
is what it's all about,
what makes clocks turn
and the sunsets come
true and without complication.

That doesn't mean lying close
in shut-up rooms
or staying always face to face.

It's meant to cover walking,
being apart and knowing
that coming back together
makes small distances even smaller.

And taking time to love
is, most of all, caring enough
to not hold on too tightly
and yet not run too loose.

DECLARATION OF MARRIAGE   [DM 4]

Celebrant to the guests: Ladies and Gentlemen,
David and *Linda* have declared before all of us that they will
live together in marriage. They have made special promises to
each other. They have symbolised it by joining hands, taking
vows, and by giving a ring (*or* by exchanging rings).

So, therefore, on your behalf and on behalf of the community, I now declare them to be husband and wife.

The bride and groom kiss.

THE SIGNING

The register and the marriage certificate are signed. The celebrant presents the couple (properly the bride, according to tradition) with the certificate.

This concludes the ceremony, and all the proceedings for the celebrant.

3 Alternatives (for Weddings)

- Introductions
- Giving Away/Presenting of the Bride
- The Asking
- Vows (including symbolic acts, and a renewal of vows)
- Readings

Introduction/sections of introduction

CAROLYN and PHIL   [WI 5]

Celebrant: *Carolyn* and *Phil* have decided to seal their marriage with this wedding, so on their behalf I welcome you today.

In their relationship they have reached the conviction that they are for each other. They see this commitment as a serious occasion, they approach it with a sense of reverence, but also with joy and happiness.

Real love between a man and a woman is perhaps the highest experience that is possible for humankind. Such love reduces selfishness, deepens personalities, but above all gives life new purpose and meaning.

We are here because *Phil* and *Carolyn* do not, and cannot, live in isolation. The experience of their love touches all of us, and it is fitting that we should celebrate their happiness. This wedding gives public recognition to the private experience of their love. At a different level we share in it, we rejoice for them, and we support them.

Though marriage means the greatest possible intimacy between two people, yet this closeness should not diminish but stimulate each partner to grow as an individual. A responsibility of each marriage partner is to be the guardian and encourager of the other's need to be alone, to develop their own talents and qualities.

It is from the balance of individuality and union that 'Love', as Khoren Arisian says, 'whose incredible strength is equal only to its incredible fragility, is born and reborn'.

Carolyn and *Phil* know that a relationship of real love can never be taken for granted, but can only survive and grow when both lovers maintain the will to openly and sensitively develop their relationship as equals. It is in this spirit that they now stand before us.

MIMI and *LONG* [WI 6]

Celebrant: Marriage is for the companionship, help, consideration and love which husband and wife ought to have for each other. Within its framework of commitment and loyalty, marriage enables the establishment of a home where, through tolerance, patience and courage, the love and affection of a man and a woman may develop into a deep and lasting relationship.

Long and *Mimi* have honoured us by inviting us to be present with them during this time. What they mean to each other is obvious. Their commitment to each other has been made for some time. They are adult. They have chosen to live together. Their choice is responsible, free, independent and happy.

Of all the men and women they know, they have chosen each other, to journey through life together.

MALCOLM and ANIKA [WI 7]

Celebrant: Throughout history there have been great love stories. There are tales of men and women who have been through great suffering, through terrible conflicts, who have overcome seemingly insurmountable barriers to be with one another.

Every love story in its own way has a certain greatness, a certain sublimity. There is often the untold history of physical and mental hardship, the fear and agony of difficult decision making, the shattering darkness of the great breaks in life's pattern, and then almost unbelievably, the 'light at the end of the tunnel'.

'True love', tradition tells us, 'never runs smooth.' But there does come a time when the forces who have sought to destroy, admit defeat and disintegrate, and love triumphs.

This is a happy occasion when *Malcolm* and *Anika* stand before us today to declare and celebrate their love and their marriage. Their path, like the many to whom I have, in general, referred, has not been easy. Perhaps, because of this they value their commitment and their happiness, and indeed this wedding, much more than had it been otherwise. They know that they can never take their relationship for granted. They know that they have found in each other that unique, yet mysterious, quality whereby they know that they are meant for each other. They know too with the poet that 'True love comes but once'.

Love, in human life, is acknowledged by all, but it eludes all defining and explanation. Only the poets dare comment.

When we think about this union between *Anika* and *Malcolm* today we take a certain heart. In the midst of the selfishness, the competition and the ambition of modern life love intrudes and exerts its inexplicable and extraordinary softening influence. This marriage encourages all of us because when a man and a woman find joy and happiness in giving and caring, in co-operating and compromising, it says something to all of us. If we recognise that life at its deepest and most personal must be selfless and loving to bring human happiness, then so it must be in the wider community of all the world.

It is to celebrate *Malcolm* and *Anika*'s love, to be influenced by it, and to take it in our lives to others, that we have all assembled here today.

LILLIAN and *JUSTIN*   [WI 8]
(Celebrant, Carol Astbury)

Celebrant to the guests: It is one of life's richest surprises when the accidental meeting of two individuals leads them to proceed together along a common path. It is indeed one of life's finest experiences when a chance relationship grows into a permanent bond of love. This meeting and this growing are what bring us together today.

The uniting in marriage of these two friends to establish a new family is an important and memorable event. It brings together two separate families and backgrounds, and creates a union that is a sign of hope in the midst of a sometimes intolerant society.

In their love for each other, which they publicly express in this ceremony, *Justin* and *Lillian* demonstrate not only their joy in the present but their commitment to share the future together. This is a time of celebration for all of us who know and love them.

Celebrant: *Justin* and *Lillian*,
As you know, no minister, no rabbi, no public official can do more than bless or solemnise your marriage. Only you can make your marriage lasting and meaningful. By a mutual commitment to creating an atmosphere of care, consideration and respect, by a willingness to face the tensions and anxieties that underlie human life, you can make your wedded life a source of great strength and joy. Your love for one another and your willingness to accept each other's strong points and weaknesses with understanding and respect will provide a foundation for continued growth and intimacy.

Respect and celebrate with each other, not only all that you have in common but also your individual perspectives on life, and the different traditions you bring with you. Cherish every opportunity that allows you to share your beliefs and grow closer to each other.

Today there is a vast unknown future stretching out before you. That future, with its hopes and disappointments, its joys and its sorrows, is hidden from your eyes, but it is a great tribute to your faith in each other that you are willing to face it together.

May the love with which you join heart and hand today never fail, but grow deeper and surer with every year you spend together.

May you dare to dream dreams not yet dreamt.

May you find constant reward and challenge as you pursue the ongoing adventure of learning who you are and where you want to go.

May you always have a special sense of your mission in life together, and may you never tire of the endless possibilities of exploring your shared existence.

MAIKO and *DIMITRI* [WI 9]
(Celebrant, John Hill)

A special introduction for a couple from two different cultures; this introduction could be easily adapted.

Celebrant: This is an extremely, sacred moment. You have set time aside. There is in these moments a tenderness and a sensitivity that will bring us out of the normal flow of life. You are here for a reason. You have come arrayed in the best of attire.

It is a time for stepping out of our routines so that we can touch something essential in life. We seek ceremony when we feel something special and profound is happening.

We do things in ceremony that are profoundly symbolic. It allows the depth of what we feel to shine through. Ceremony is that visible means for honoring that unseen world that we feel within.

Marriage is not only linking our lives to another individual. We are entering a myth that goes deep into our heart. The happiness that *Dimitri* and *Maiko* embrace today contains many wishes, for they will be able to explore and enter into the mystery of who they are. The happiness that they hope for in marriage embraces the spoken and the unspoken wishes for fulfilment. What they offer to each other is the opportunity to explore, enter and fulfil notions of who they are and what they can be.

In one sense marriage is not fundamentally the relationship between two people, but rather an entry into into a destiny, an opening to the potential life that lies hidden from view until evoked by the particular thoughts and feelings of marriage. That is why it is so important that you are all here.

★

Here is an example of a personal history introduction based on the questions in chapter 1.

MARK and *SYLVIA*   [WI 10]

Celebrant: I call upon everyone here present to be a fellow-witness with me in this marriage we are about to celebrate between Mark and Sylvia. We are here, not only to witness their commitment to each other but our presence here means that we wish them well and every happiness for their life together.

The history of Sylvia and Mark goes back to 1987 when they were introduced by a mutual friend, Rory Sheridan, at an after-work lawyers' Friday drinks-and-dinner get-together. They were initially attracted each to the other. Mark even got to the stage of starting to dial Sylvia's number, but his courage failed him, and he hung up.

But whether or not you believe in fate, this marriage was meant to be. By this time Mark had left the legal eagles of the Premier's Department and was working in education. His colleague, Shane Finnegan, decided he needed a legal officer, and Sylvia got the job.

Sylvia and Mark were surprised to meet each other again. With a great deal of pleasure, Anton showed her around, and the former chemistry was reactivated from that moment. What they found in their work life was that they got on wonderfully well together. However, they did not court each other in the obvious way. Discreet meetings and impulsive trysts of a most respectable kind were arranged.

The interaction reached a definitive point when Sylvia remarked that she went walking every Sunday. Mark, too legally moulded by fears of sexual harassment to ask Sylvia out directly, suggested that she ring him next time she was going for a walk on a Sunday. The next Sunday afternoon Sylvia rang, and invited him for a Sunday walk. He was there in five minutes!

This was a decisive moment — Sylvia had taken the initiative. All cultural and legal safety precautions had been observed, and a Sunday walk, followed by an 'el cheapo' Victoria Street Vietnamese meal, added to the moment and sealed this day of consequence.

It was only a matter of time before they shifted in with one another, bought a house together, and grew closer and closer. They feel very comfortable with one another, and although they have some differences they know they are on the same level of shared interests and values.

Mark loves and admires Sylvia because she is positive, optimistic, good-natured, caring about people, affectionate, considerate of the people in her life. She is intelligent and organised in a way that he admires. She 'jumps out of bed in the morning with a smile on her face'. He also likes the look of her, and everything about her style as an individual.

Sylvia loves and admires Mark because of his enthusiasm, his sincerity, his intelligence, the integrity of his character and because he is a man of principles and standards. She also likes the way he strives for perfection, and painstakingly and pedantically works to get things right — that he is a seeker of perfection. She particularly loves him because he is generous and affectionate.

Mark's and Sylvia's commitment has obviously been made for some time, but the purpose of this marriage today is to publicly celebrate this commitment with you, their close family and friends from every stage of their lives. Every one of you here today is here because you are special people to Sylvia and Mark. They call on you today, in a formal way, to accept their decision and to call on your support.

There is a note of sadness today. Sylvia's father, Marcel, died some weeks ago. He was delighted at the prospect of this marriage, and we do think of him on this occasion. He gave

Mark and Sylvia valuable advice — he thought it was important that they give each other space to follow individual interests. Relationships should not confine but allow independence. Mark and Sylvia have heeded this advice. They see their future together as one of loving mutual assistance, encouragement and support. They see this relationship as enriching each other's lives. Today they want to communicate their happiness to you.

Giving Away/Presentation of the Bride (both parents)

RICHARD AND SUZETTE [GA 5]

Celebrant to the guests: Who brings this man to stand beside this woman?

Groom's parents: We do.

Celebrant to the guests: Who brings this woman to stand beside this man?

Bride's parents: We do.

Celebrant: Are you willing now and always to support and strengthen this marriage by upholding both *Susette* and *Richard* with your love and support?

All parents: We are.

The Asking

ALEELA and **ZAFIR** [A 7]

Celebrant: *Aleela* and *Zafir*,
Do you come here freely, and without reservation,
to enter a relationship as companions living together as husband and wife, enjoying equality?
Do you promise to love, respect,

assist and look after each other
for the rest of your lives?
Are you prepared to live in harmony,
and jointly strive for the welfare of your family,
and for a just and equal society?

Vows

Many couples decide to write their own vows. Here are some personal vows.

JULIE and ANDREW　　　　　　　　　　　　　　　　[WV 5]

Andrew: *Julie,*
　　I am proud to take you as my wife.

　　For all of the time we have been together
　　there has always been the kind of love and understanding
　　that is only shared when there is true love.
　　You have helped me triumph over challenges presented,
　　encouraged my personal growth and boosted my
　　　　self-esteem.
　　You have helped me become the person I am today,
　　and with your help I will be a better man tomorrow than
　　　　I was yesterday.

　　I love the way you love and care for me,
　　I love the way you trust and believe in me,
　　I love the way you always look your best for me,
　　I love you, and I love my life with you.
　　Today, as we begin our lives as husband and wife,
　　I commit myself to you.

Julie: *Andrew,*
　　I take you as my husband.

　　To say I love you is not enough,
　　to try to condense the depth of my feelings into a few
　　　　words is impossible;
　　it doesn't tell of the respect I have for you as an individual,
　　nor how I appreciate how tender and caring you are,
　　nor the joy I find in your laughter,

nor the tears I hold back for your pain,
nor the strength you give when I need it,
nor the pleasure I feel in your touch.

But if to say 'I love you' means all these things,
then let me say, 'I love you more each day'.

DEREK and PHILIPPA   [WV 6]
(Celebrant, Carol Astbury)

Derek:

I, *Derek*, offer myself to you, *Philippa*,
to be your husband,
your friend, your lover and your lifelong companion;
to share my life with yours;
to build our dreams together,
to support you through times of trouble,
and rejoice with you in times of happiness;
to treat you with respect, love and loyalty
through all the trials and triumphs of our lives together.
This commitment is made in love,
kept in faith, lived in hope,
and eternally made new.

Philippa:

I am honoured to accept you as my husband.

I, *Philippa*, offer myself to you, *Derek*, to be your wife,
your friend, your lover and your lifelong companion;
to share my life with yours;
to build our dreams together;
to support you through times of trouble;
and rejoice with you in times of happiness;
to treat you with respect, love and loyalty
through all the trials and triumphs of our lives together.
This commitment is made in love,
kept in faith, lived in hope,
and eternally made new.

Derek: I am honoured to accept you as my wife.

DANIELLE and KARL   [WV 7]

In this commitment ceremony the couple decided read each alternating verse in the poem instead of the usual vows:

Groom: [WV 18]

I promise to give you the best of myself,
and to ask of you no more than you can give

Bride:

I promise to accept you the way you are.
I fell in love with you for the qualities, abilities,
and outlook on life that you have,
and I won't try to reshape you in a different image.

Groom:

I promise to respect you as a person
with your own interests, desires, and needs,
and to realise that these are sometimes different,
but no less important, than my own.

Bride:

I promise to share with you my time,
my close attention,
and to bring joy and strength and imagination
to our relationship.

Groom:

I promise to keep myself open to you,
to let you see through the window of my personal world,
into my innermost fears and feelings, secrets and dreams.

Bride:

I promise to grow along with you,
to be willing to face change, as we both change,
in order to keep our relationship alive and exciting.

Groom:

And finally, I promise to love you as your husband,
in good times and in bad with all I have to give,
and all that I feel inside,
in the only way I know how,
completely and forever.

Bride:

> And finally, I promise to love you as your wife,
> in good times and in bad with all I have to give,
> and all that I feel inside,
> in the only way I know how,
> completely and forever.

VICKY and PIETRO [WV 8]

Pietro:

> I, *Pietro*, take you, *Vicky*, to be my wife.
> I hereby give voice to my soul
> in the offering of my most heartfelt pledge to you.
> I swear neither trials nor time shall prove false this oath,
> nor lessen my resolve.
> I promise of myself my faith, devotion,
> and above all else, my undying love,
> that we may share and grow together for all our lives.

LAN and MIKE [WV 9]

Lan: *Mike,*

> I come to you in marriage with great joy and excitement
> in my heart. I feel honoured to be loved by such a kind,
> generous person, a man who can ask much of love and
> gives endlessly in return, a man who never lets me go
> unchallenged.
>
> May we love one another with constancy, live joyously,
> laugh freely, and support our marriage through the trials
> and triumphs to come.
>
> Today I promise to try to always be kind to you, to lean
> on you when I should, and to be the best person I know
> how to be. When you need strength, I will offer mine.
>
> When you need words of encouragement, I will listen
> and provide support.
>
> I make these vows with complete faith that we can
> make a wonderful life together.
>
> I declare my love for you and my desire to be with you
> always as husband and wife. I choose you above all others
> to share my life. I will honour this promise as long as we
> both shall live.

JAMES and CATHERINE [WV 10]

James: *Catherine,*

Catherine,
I come to you in marriage with great joy and excitement in my heart.

Your love and patience over the past seven years have shaped me into the person I am today.

In my eyes you are the most beautiful person in the world.

I look forward to facing the challenges of love, marriage, and family life together with you.

I declare my love for you and my desire to be with you always as husband and wife. I choose you above all others to share my life. I will honour this promise as long as we both shall live.

IMRAN and SASHA [WV 11]

I, *Imran/Sasha*, call upon the persons here present to witness that I take you, *Sasha/Imran*, to be my lawful *wife/-husband*.

HENRIK and JENNY [WV 12]

Henrik/Jenny, I want to be with you always just as you are. I choose you, above all others, to share my life with me in marriage. I love you for yourself, and I want you to become all that you can be. I promise to honour this pledge as long as I live.

VIRGINIA and EDWARD [WV 13]

I, *Virginia/Edward*, take you, *Edward/Virginia*, as my spouse, my lifelong partner.
I will do everything I can to maintain our love.
I will talk to you and listen to you. I will give to you and I will take from you.
Your success and happiness will be mine.

Homosexual/Gay Commitment Ceremony

Gay marriages have not yet been recognised in law, but to the gay couples concerned their commitment to each other is the same as in any heterosexual ceremony. There is very little difference to the other wedding ceremonies in this book, simply substitute the words 'spouse' or 'partner' for 'wife/husband'.

GAVIN and JEREMY   [V 15]

Gavin:
> *Jeremy*, I want to be with you always just as you are.
> I choose you above all others to share my life with me.
> I love you for yourself,
> and I want you to become all that you can be.
> I promise to honour this pledge as long as I live.

Jeremy:
> *Gavin*, I want to be with you always just as you are.
> I choose you above all others to share my life with me.
> I love you for yourself,
> and I want you to become all that you can be.
> I promise to honour this pledge as long as I live.

★

Why not take sentences and phrases from every vow in this book, perhaps incorporate some of your own, and put your own vows together?

Ring Ceremonies

VUTHY and SOKHA   [RC 5]

Groom and the bride:
> We will wear these rings,
> and the world will know
> that I am yours,
> and you are mine.

JANE **and** *CHRIS* [RC 6]

Bride, as she accepts the ring: *Chris,*
> I thank you for this beautiful ring,
> I accept it as a symbol that I belong to you.
> This ring will remind me of you,
> I will wear it with love,
> all my life.

This is repeated for the groom if rings are exchanged.

★

Many traditional ceremonies are accompanied by symbolic acts, such as those following.

Sharing of Wine

ROBERT **and** *MICHAELA* [S 1]

The groom pours a glass of wine, and both bride and groom drink from it.

Celebrant: The glass of wine is symbolic of the cup of life. As you share this wine, you promise to share all that the future may bring. All the sweetness the cup of life may hold for you should be sweeter because you drink it together; and whatever drops of bitterness it may contain should be less because they are shared. We wish you all the blessings that life can bring — joy and gladness, love and companionship, happiness and prosperity all the days of your life.

Breaking the Glass

DAVID **and** *SARAH* [S 2]

Celebrant: Following the Jewish tradition of *David*'s family, and indeed for all of us who share the values of Western culture, I ask you, *David*, to break this glass according to tradition.
> The breaking of the glass symbolises the fragility of life

and love. It is a sign of good fortune, and a hope that your love remains as true and as pure as it is at this moment.

The glass is wrapped in a cloth, and the groom breaks the glass by stamping on it with his foot.

Support Vows of the Guests   [WV 15]

Celebrant: Friends, *Angela* and *Will* have asked that all of you, who have been so important in their relationship and their individual lives, now pledge to support their marriage in the same way as you have supported them as single people. *Will* and *Angela* can sometimes be quite competitive, so they ask you as a group to henceforth do all you can to support the marriage, and not so much the individuals.

Please show your support by responding to the following vows with the words 'We will'.

Will you pledge to support *Angela* and *Will* as a couple in their marriage rather than as individuals?

All: We will.

Celebrant: Will you support them in their new life together, rejoicing in their happiness and sustaining them in their struggles?

All: We will.

Celebrant: Will you be patient and forgiving when they make mistakes or cause pain?

All: We will.

(There are many possible variations for these vows.)

Candle-lighting Ceremonies

JAMES and *MARLENE*   [S 3]
(Celebrant: Kathleen Hurley)

Celebrant: Before *James* and *Marlene* make their marriage vows to each other, they will light their marriage candle.

Marlene and *James*, take these candles. These candles represent each of you as unique individuals.

The celebrant indicates the individual candles, which are then lit.

Celebrant: The flame in each burns with the warmth and love that your family and friends have fostered in each of you.

The marriage candle is then lit simultaneously by the two individual candles.

Celebrant: As you join the two candles together to light the single marriage candle, the flame flares higher than before. This flame of love symbolises how *James's* and *Marlene's* lives will be richer in their union.

The united flame is a strong symbol. It represents the warmth of their love the sacredness of their relationship, and the light that will guide them through everyday of their future together.

GEORGINA and BEN   [S 4]

The groom lights a candle, which is then held jointly by the bride and groom.

Celebrant: Just as a flame from a candle is used to light another candle and the first candle is not diminished by this act of giving, soo too love, when it is shared, never diminishes the giver but always warms the receiver of the love.

The lighting of the candle is a ceremonial acknowledgement of the vows exchanged by *Georgina* and *Ben* that have united them in marriage. This single flame signifies that marriage is a joining of two people who have chosen to share a life together rather than individual lives.

The light from the candle is a beacon that will guide and protect them. Each year, on their wedding anniversary, by relighting the candle they will be able to relive and remember the vows that they, in all solemnity, have made today.

The Lighted Candle   [WR 19]

The lighted candle close entwines
Two hearts in love together,
Friendships dearest pledge is made
In joy forever.

United you shall walk through life
Sharing earth's pain and pleasure,
Hand in hand you shall strive
For achievement in life together.

Should the path be rough and thorny
Let love sustain and guide you,
Should the way be strewn with roses
Let the joy of life sustain you.

> *Traditional* (adapted from the
> silk ribbon ribbon custom)

The bride extinguishes the candle, and hands it to the celebrant.

Stepparents and Stepchildren

Society must now face the challenge of working out guidelines, conventions of behaviour and principles of morality in stepparent/stepchild relationships. A good beginning to a mutually rewarding relationship can start within the marriage ceremony — if it is considered appropriate and everyone is comfortable about it. One of the many ways children and stepchildren can be included in a ceremony follows.

BERNARD AND *BRETT*   [SV 1]
Celebrant: Ladies and Gentlemen,
Today *Bernard* marries *Lydia*. But we all know that it this isn't the only relationship established today. There is a whole new network of relationships set up by this marriage, as there is in any marriage. Perhaps the most important family relationship that is now established is that between *Bernard* and *Brett*, *Lydia's* son.

Step relationships are often difficult for all sorts of reasons, but with the right attitude, as we all know, they can be very helpful and productive.

So I ask you, *Bernard*, will you do your best to assist *Brett* in whatever way you can during these important years of growth? Will you respect his relationship with his parents, yet be aware of your important place in his life and treat him with interest, care, concern, fairness and respect?

Bernard: I will.

Celebrant: *Brett*, now that your family will include *Bernard* as a parent to you, will you treat him with respect and fairness, and do your best to have the best and friendliest relationship possible?

Brett: I will.

Procession of the Families

The groom's family and friends assembled in one corner of the Fitzroy Gardens (a spacious public park and garden in Melbourne). On the diagonal corner, about a kilometre away, the bride's family and friends assembled.

Pied Piper of Hamelin style each group was led by a musician: a clarinet for the groom, a violin for the bride. Both families, accompanied by music, met at midpoint, at the lake and fountain where the celebrant waited, and the ceremony began.

The symbolism was wonderful, for it was clear that it was not just two persons but two families, two networks of people, coming together.

Renewal of Vows

Reaffirmation or renewal of vows ceremonies are also suitable for married couples, who, after separation, are reunited. Some also feel the need for such a ceremony when their original wedding ceremony, for one reason or another, was meaningless to them (they may have been too young, had no say in the ceremony, or cannot remember any of it). The most common reason is to reaffirm the marriage on the occasion of an anniversary.

These ceremonies are arranged exactly the same as marriage ceremonies. There is one difference, however, which is extremely important. Each introduction must be unique. It is best for the couple to spend an hour or two with the celebrant discussing the ceremony and why they wish to have it. The couple or the celebrant should then write the introduction so that it expresses their views and feelings accurately. If this is not done, the ceremony may not be successful. I also advise writing personal renewal of vows.

All the elements of marriage ceremonies given in chapters 1 to 3 are suitable for renewal of vows. It must be clear that this ceremony is a *renewal*, not a marriage (it is a serious legal offence in any system to pretend to officiate at a marriage ceremony when, in fact, it is not such a ceremony).

GEOFF AND MARGARET [WV 15]

Celebrant: *Geoff* and *Margaret*,
Today is your twenty-fifth wedding anniversary — your silver celebration. Your main responsibility to bring up your children is now over, and tonight, when you renew and reaffirm your marriage vows to each other, you can happily look back on the achievement of raising a family, and at the same time you can look forward to a new era in your life.

It will be a time, we hope, when you can concentrate on developing your love for each other, freer than you have been from the tensions and hassles that characterise the struggle to become established in life and in nurturing a growing family.

Tonight is a night when you reassure each other, and expressing deep loyalty and loving trust as the basis of your marriage relationship.

Both of you believe in marriage — in the fullness of the husband and wife relationship — and you know that a deep bond unites you both. It must do so because of what you have been through together; all the stresses and tensions of the past have not weakened your love, but have only made you more determined to stick by each other. This relationship is, and must be, very deep. As the poet, contemplating and comparing the rush of life to the plunge of the great waterfalls, says: 'Deep calls to deep in the roar of your cataracts'.

Your relationship, I know, is as important to you as life itself. Tonight's recommitment should encourage you both to be more dedicated to each other so that you can look forward to a settled and enjoyable future.

(A selection of readings and symbolic acts follows.)

Geoff: Twenty-five years ago, I, *Geoff*, took you, *Margaret*, to be my lawful wife, to have and to hold, from that day forward, for better, for worse, for richer, for poorer, in sickness and in health.

This day I reaffirm that vow.

Margaret: Twenty-five years ago, I, *Margaret*, took you, *Geoff*, to be my lawful husband, to have and to hold from that day forward, for better, for worse, for richer, for poorer, in sickness and in health.

This day I reaffirm that vow.

Geoff: *Margaret*,
With this ring
I reaffirm that we are wed,
Take and wear it
As a pledge of my love,
And as a symbol
Of all we have shared
And all that we shall share.

Wife to repeat for husband, if wished.

Readings chosen by the couple are then read. (Wedding readings are easily adapted for this ceremony.)

Celebrant: Ladies and Gentlemen,
Geoff and *Margaret* have declared before me,
and before all of you, their relatives and friends,

that they will continue to live together in marriage.
They have made special promises to each other.
They have symbolised it by joining hands, taking vows,
and by *Geoff* giving *Margaret* a ring.

I therefore call upon all present here today
to be fellow-witnesses with me to this reaffirmation.
I declare that they have been, and will remain,
husband and wife.

Readings

Short readings give balance and effect to parts of a ceremony.
For example, one is often used just after rings have been
placed to emphasise the meaning of that event.

From The Song of Songs [WR 20]

Set me as a seal upon your arm,
As a seal upon your heart,
For love is as strong as death.
Many waters cannot quench it,
No flood can sweep it away.

A Birthday [WR 21]

My heart is like a singing bird
Whose nest is in a watered shoot;
My heart is like an apple-tree
Whose boughs are bent with thickset fruit;
My heart is like a rainbow shell
That paddles in a halcyon sea;
My heart is gladder than all these
Because my love has come to me.

Raise me a dais of silk and down;
Hang it with vair and purple dyes;
Carve it in doves and pomegranates,
And peacocks with a hundred eyes;
Work it in gold and silver grapes,

In leaves and silver fleurs-de-lys;
Because the birthday of my life
Is come, my love is come to me.

Christina Rossetti

To a Marriage   [WR 22]

In your hands you hold the key to life,
The key to open up the door of love,
The strength to face together joy or strife,
And all of human frailties rise above.

You take a vow this day to be as one
In all you do — in all that you aspire,
And let there be no one beneath the sun
Who'd seek to put asunder your desire.

And let us wish this knot we tie this day
Be firm and strong against the test of time,
And let our children's children say
That all was good and right and fine.

And so in all humility and in this place
We cast your love into the hands of fate,
For it is written true that all you face,
If faced with love, you'll triumph and be great.

For greatness lies within the souls of lovers,
There is no power can tear it from your grasp,
It bonds your hearts as one, to one another's,
As Alpha and Omega — first and last.

So go you forward from this place this day,
And as you journey along the road of life
Know that you stand together, come what may,
For true love comes just once, not twice, not thrice.

Brian Zouch

From Romance   [WR 23]

I will make you brooches and toys for your delight,
Of bird-song at morning and star-shine at night.

I will make a palace fit for you and me,
Of green days in forests and blue days at sea.

And this shall be for music when no one else is near,
The fine song for singing, the rare song to hear!
That only I remember, that only you admire,
Of the broad road that stretches and the roadside fire.

Robert Louis Stevenson

Love's Philosophy [WR 24]

The fountains mingle with the river,
And the rivers with the ocean,
The winds of heaven mix for ever
With a sweet emotion;

Nothing in the world is single;
All things by a law divine
In one another's being mingle
Why not I with thine?

See the mountains kiss high heaven,
And the waves clasp one another;
No sister flower would be forgiven
If it disdained its brother;

And the sunlight clasps the earth,
And the moonbeams kiss the sea,
What are all these kissings worth,
If thou kiss not me?

Percy Bysshe Shelley

From The Good-Morrow [WR 25]

I wonder by my troth, what thou, and I
Did, till we lov'd? were we not wean'd till then?
But suck'd on country pleasures, childishly?
Or snorted we i' the seven sleepers den?
T'was so: But this, all pleasures fancies be.
If ever any beauty I did see,
Which I desir'd, and got, t'was but a dream of thee.

John Donne

Adapted from 1 Corinthians 13 [WR 26]

Love is always patient and kind;
It is never jealous;
Love is never boastful or conceited;
It is never rude or selfish;
It does not take offence,
And is not resentful.

Love takes no pleasure
In other people's faults
But delights in the truth;
It is always ready to excuse, to trust, to hope.
It is always ready to endure whatever comes.
Finally, true love does not come to an end.

To Anthea [WR 27]

Oh, bid me love, and I will give
A loving heart to thee.
A heart as soft, a heart as kind,
A heart as sound and free,
As in the whole world thou canst find,
That heart I'll give to thee.

Robert Herrick

From The Prophet [WR 28]

Love one another,
But make not a bond of love.
Let it rather be a moving sea
Between the shores of your souls.

Fill each other's cup
But drink not from the same cup.
Sing and dance together and be joyous,
But let each one of you be alone,
Even as the strings of a lute are alone
Though they quiver with the same music.

Give your hearts,
But not into each other's keeping,
For only the hand of life
Can contain your hearts.

And stand together
Yet not too near together:
For the pillars of the temple stand apart,
And the oak tree and the cypress
Grow not in each other's shadow.

Kahlil Gibran

A Red, Red Rose   [WR 29]

O my Love's like a red, red rose
That's newly sprung in June;
O my Love's like the melodie
That's sweetly play'd in tune.

As fair art thou, my bonnie lass,
So deep in love am I;
And I will love thee still, my Dear,
Till a' the seas gang dry:

Till a' the seas gang dry, my Dear,
And the rocks melt wi' the sun;
I will love thee still, my Dear
While the sands o' life shall run.

Robert Burns

How Do I Love Thee?   [WR 30]

How do I love thee? Let me count the ways.
I love thee to the depth and breadth and height
My soul can reach, when feeling out of sight
For the ends of Being and ideal Grace.

I love thee to the level of every day's
Most quiet need, by sun and candle light.
I love thee freely, as men strive for Right;

I love thee purely, as they turn from Praise.

I love thee with the passion put to use
In my old griefs, and with my childhood's faith.
I love thee with a love I seemed to lose
With my lost saints — I love thee with the breath,
Smiles, tears, of all my life! — and, if God choose,
I shall but love thee better after death.

Elizabeth Barrett Browning

If We Wanted To [WR 31]

Our love is strengthened by knowing that
each of us could survive on our own
if we wanted to —
but realizing that more than anything —
we choose to be together.

As Long as Your Eyes Are Blue [WR 32]

Wilt thou love me, sweet, when my hair is grey,
And my cheeks shall have lost their hue?
When the charms of youth shall have passed away
Will your love as of old prove true?

For the locks may change and the heart may range,
And the love be no longer fond:
Wilt thou love me with truth in the years of youth
And away to the years beyond?
Oh, I love you, sweet, for your locks of brown
And the blush on your cheek that lies —
But I love you most for the kindly heart
That I see in your sweet blue eyes —

For the eyes are the signs of the soul within,
Of the heart that is real and true,
And mine own sweetheart, I shall love you still,
Just as long as your eyes are blue.

For the locks may bleach, and the cheeks of peach
May be reft of their golden hue;
But mine own sweetheart, I shall love you still,
Just as long as your eyes are blue.

A. B. (Banjo) Paterson

Love   [WR 33]

Love,
puts the music in laughter,
the beauty in song,
the warmth in a shoulder,
the gentle in strong.

Love,
puts the magic in memories,
the sunshine in skies,
the gladness in giving,
the starlight in eyes.

Love,
puts the fun in together,
the sad in apart,
the hope in tomorrow,
the joy in the heart.

Rod McKuen

Every Two Unique   [WR 34]

No human relationship gives one possession of another. A relationship links two people together. Each person is unique and different so the mode and style of this linking varies. But whether it is friendship or love, the two people, side by side, find and achieve so much together, which one of them cannot find or achieve alone.

In a relationship the lover recognises the talent and the beauty of the other. They should tell the other of it when they see it. In a relationship, if you accept the sunshine and warmth, you must also be prepared to accept the overcast and the cool.

Among intelligent people the surest basis for the relationship of marriage is friendship — the sharing of real interests — the ability to work through issues together, to work towards common goals together, and to understand and share each others' thoughts and dreams.

Thomas Davidson

love [WR 35]

love is more thicker than forget
more thinner than recall
more seldom than a wave is wet
more frequent than to fail

it is most mad and moonly
and less it shall unbe
than all the sea which only
is deeper than the sea

love is less always than to win
less never than alive
less bigger than the least begin
less littler than forgive

it is more sane and sunly
and more it cannot die
than all the sky which only
is higher than the sky

e. e. cummings

To My Wife [WR 36]

Upon this day I pledge my all
to you and only you,
and never shall love's blossom fall
through any act I do.

My love for you is pure and strong,
my eye for you alone,
I take your hand and guide you on,
in each our hearts a home.

This boundless love I have for you
I give in charge this day,
that you shall know, all others too,
'tis not a game I play.

From this day on, we wedded live,
two lives to be as one,
this gift of love to you I give
to never be undone.

So journey on life's road with me
and say for all to know,
our love is deeper than the sea,
and yet has much to grow.

Brian Zouch

From The Passionate Shepherd to His Love [WR 37]

Come live with me, and be my love,
And we will all the pleasures prove,
That valleys, groves, hills and fields,
Woods, or steepy mountain yields.

And we will sit upon the rocks,
Seeing the shepherds feed their flocks,
By shallow rivers, to whose falls
Melodious birds sing madrigals.

And I will make thee beds of roses,
And a thousand fragrant posies,
A cap of flowers, and a kirtle
Embroider'd all with leaves of myrtle;

A gown made of the finest wool,
Which from our pretty lambs we pull;
Fair lined slippers for the cold,
With buckles of the purest gold.

A belt of straw and ivy buds,
With coral clasps and amber studs.
And if these pleasures may thee move,
Come live with me, and be my love.

Christopher Marlowe

A Marriage   [WR 38]

A marriage —
makes of two fractional lives a whole,
gives to two purposeless lives a work,
and doubles the strength of each to perform it;
It gives it two questioning natures

a reason for living and something to live for;
It will give a new gladness to the sunshine,
a new fragrance to the flowers,
a new beauty to the earth,
and a new mystery to life.

Mark Twain

To My Dear and Loving Husband [WR 39]

If ever two were one, then surely we;
If ever man were lov'd by wife, then thee;
If ever wife was happy in a man,
Compare with me, ye women, if you can.

I prize thy love more than whole mines of gold,
Or all the riches that the east doth hold.
My love is such that rivers cannot quench,
Nor ought but love from thee, give recompence.

Thy love is such I can no way repay,
The heavens reward thee manifold, I pray.
Then while we live, in love let's persevere,
That when we live no more, we may live ever.

Anne Bradstreet

My Friend [WR 40]

I love you
not only for what you are
but for what I am
when I am with you.

I love you
not only for what
you have made of yourself
but for what you are making of me.

I love you
because you have done more
than any creed could have done

to make me good, and more
than any fate could have done
to make me happy.
You have done it without a touch,
without a word
without a sign.
You have done it
by being yourself.

The Art of Marriage [WR 41]

A good marriage must be created.
In the art of marriage the little things are the big
    things —

It is never being too old to hold hands.
It is remembering to say 'I love you' at least once
    each day.
It is never going to sleep angry.
It is having a mutual sense of values and common
    objectives.
It is standing together facing the world.
It is forming a circle of love that gathers in the whole
    family.
It is speaking words of appreciation and demonstrating
    gratitude in thoughtful ways.
It is having the capacity to forgive and forget.
It is giving each other an atmosphere in which each can
    grow.
It is finding room for the things of the spirit.
It is a common search for the good and the beautiful.
It is not only marrying the right partner —
It is being the right partner

We Two [WR 42]

You and I have so much love
that it burns like a fire,
in which we bake a lump of clay,

moulded into a figure of you
and a figure of me.

We take both of them
and break them into pieces,
and mix the pieces with water,
and mould again.
a figure of you and a figure of me.

I am in your clay,
You are in my clay.

Kuan Tao-Sheng

Love One Another   [WR 43]

If you can love each other through the sunshine and the
    storm
And keep the flame of true devotion glowing bright and
    warm,
If you can give each other room to grow and change and
    learn,
Yet still hold one another close in mutual concern,
If you can be both lovers and the very best of friends,
And face together hand in hand the challenges life sends,
If you can offer patience, comfort and real understanding,
Encourage one another's efforts, yet be understanding,
If you can show true love and faith in everything you do,
Then married life will surely hold much joy for both
    of you.

May the Road Rise Up to Meet You   [WR 44]

May the road rise up to meet you,
May the wind be always at your back,
May the sun shine warm upon your face,
And the rains fall soft on your fields.

May you have warm words on a cold evening,
A full moon on a dark night,
May the roof above you never fall in,
And the friends gathered below never fall out.

May you never be in want,
And always have a soft pillow for your head,
May you be forty years in heaven
Before the devil knows you are dead.

May you be poor in misfortunes, rich in blessings,
Slow to make enemies and quick to make friends,
But be you rich or poor, quick or slow,
May you know nothing but happiness from this day on.

Traditional (Irish)

From Under Milk Wood   [WR 45]

MR EDWARDS: Myfanwy Price!

MISS PRICE: Mr Mog Edwards!

MR EDWARDS: I am a draper mad with love. I love you
more than all the flannelette and calico, candlewick,
dimity, crash and merino, tussore, cretonne, crepon,
muslin, poplin, ticking and twill in the whole Cloth
Hall of the world. I have come to take you away to my
Emporium on the hill, where the change hums on
wires. Throw away your little bedsocks and your Welsh
wool knitted jacket, I will warm the sheets like an
electric toaster, I will lie by your side like the Sunday
roast.

MISS PRICE: I will knit you a wallet of forget-me-not blue,
for the money to be comfy. I will warm your heart by
the fire so that you can slip it in under your vest when
the shop is closed.

MR EDWARDS: Myfanwy, Myfanwy, before the mice gnaw
at your bottom drawer will you say —

MISS PRICE: Yes, Mog, yes, Mog, yes, yes, yes.

MR EDWARDS: And all the bells of the tills of the town
shall ring for our wedding.

Dylan Thomas

Yes, I'll Marry You, My Dear [WR 46]

Yes, I'll marry you, my dear, and here's the reason why;
So I can push you out of bed when the baby starts to cry,
And if we hear a knocking and it's creepy and it's late,
I have you the torch you see, and you investigate.

Yes, I'll marry you, my dear, you may not apprehend it,
But when the tumble-drier goes it's you that has to
        mend it,
You have to face the neighbour should our labrador
        attack him,
And if a drunkard fondles me, it's you that has to whack
        him.

Yes, I'll marry you, my dear, you're virile and you're lean,
My house is like a pigsty, you can help to keep it clean,
That little sexy dinner which you served by candlelight,
As I just do chipolatas, you can cook it every night!

It's you who has to work the drill and put up curtain
        track,
And when I've got the PMT it's you who get the flak,
    I do see great advantages, but none of them for you,
And so before you see the light, I do, I do, I do!

Pam Ayres

★

Hundreds of other readings could have been included in this collection. English literature is immensely rich in its possibilities, so, if you have not found what you want, go on your own search — or write your own.

4 Traditions and Symbols

Something old,
Something new,
Something borrowed,
Something blue.

Symbols are signs or reminders, which, either naturally or by convention, lead our minds to truths, beliefs, or persons in our lives. In short, a symbol or a sign is something that leads to the knowledge of something else — smoke is a sign of fire, red is a sign of danger.

All aspects of life have symbols. Within weddings we have had symbols from time immemorial, we have symbols that have kept their meaning, and symbols that have changed their meaning. Some symbols have died out, and new symbols have gained favour. As marriage changes so will the symbols and customs thay surround the wedding.

Marriage by consent
The marriage between lovers (as distinct from marriage by

---

* The main source for the information in this chapter is E. Schillebeeckz, *Marriage*, vols 1 and 2, Sheed & Ward, London, 1965.

arrangement, purchase, capture or by shotgun) has had a patchy career, but now seems to be well established! I hope this book will extend people's freedom even further, not only to marry whom they like, but with the ceremony they want — and how, when, and where they like.

Arrangements between households in Greco-Roman society weakened about the fifth century BC, when marriage by mutual consent gradually gained acceptance and legal status. This was the basis of *usus* — living together for one year after their initial agreement to marry, and the origin of de facto marriage (a real marriage, but one without a ceremony).

Egypt was the first country to regard marriage as an agreement between the couple. This probably influenced the Greeks, and later paved the way for 'marriages of love'.

Over the centuries, and in various nations, the notion of consent and love has varied. Some societies still use marriage brokers, and many marriages are still 'arranged'.

In Western culture the marriage consent must precede the ceremony — otherwise the couple would not be there. We must therefore now make the distinction between the *marriage* and the *wedding* (which celebrates and/or confirms the marriage).

Joining of hands

This Roman custom (*iunctio dexterarum*) became the symbol of marriage by consent.

The espousal or betrothal

This custom used to be the actual marriage contract, though often the parties did not live together until some time later. The modern engagement comes from this arrangement, though it does not now have the force of law or the same support in our present culture. For the first half of this century a person who broke an engagement could be sued for 'breach of promise'.

Engagement ring

In ancient Mesopotamia a ring often had a seal on it. The party to a contract would press the ring-seal into the soft clay of the cuneiform tablet, thus signifying the person's binding agreement to the contract.

Another custom developed whereby a bar of gold or silver was broken in two; one piece was taken by the bride, and the other by the groom, to signify the sealing of the marriage contract.

From the Egyptians came the custom of placing the engagement and wedding rings on the third finger of the left hand. They believed that from this finger a 'vein of love' went directly to the heart — the universal symbol of love. The ring circle itself is a natural symbol of unending love: 'My love will end when the circle ends'.

At the time of the Roman Empire, betrothals were arranged by the fathers, sometimes when their children were still very young. There was no legal form to this, but it did entail, so Tertullian tells us, the giving of a pledge, which often took the form of a ring.

The first diamond engagement ring, it is said, was given by the Emperor Maximilian I to Mary of Burgundy, whom he married in 1477.

A diamond is not necessarily the only stone for an engagement ring — it is a matter of personal taste.

Many people decide to have no engagement ring at all, but to spend what money they have on a wedding ring — this being the most important symbol for them now.

The engagement (see *Espousal or betrothal*) was formerly the more definite and legal aspect of the marriage contract, and in early England rings were exchanged at this time. The engagement has now lost most of this kind of legal and cultural importance and the wedding ceremony has assumed it.

Wedding ring

Wedding rings are frequently of plain white or yellow gold. In recent years wedding rings have become more elaborate.

Now that the wedding has become much more important than the engagement, it seems appropriate to have the most valued ring for the wedding ceremony.

The use of wedding rings in modern European society

dates from earliest times, and became the custom with Christians by 860 AD.

Rings have been made of all sorts of materials — iron, steel, bronze, rush, leather, silver and gold.

Bucks' party
The tradition of this bachelors' dinner or 'bucks' party' goes back to ancient Greece, where it was known as the 'men's mess'.

Wearing of white
White was the colour for the bride to wear in both ancient Rome and Greece. It did have some association with the imitation of the vestal virgins, but was more commonly considered the colour that deterred evil spirits and was mainly worn to deter such evil demons.

In later centuries brides wore dresses of any colour, but when Queen Victoria wore a white dress for her wedding to Prince Albert it triggered the present trend of again wearing a white dress for weddings.

In my opinion, white is quite acceptable for brides who are not virgins — widows, divorcees and others. Everyone, needless to say, can do without evil spirits!

Any kind of dress in which the bride feels her true self is what is now worn or should be worn.

Bridal veil
The veil is said by some to be the symbol of the wife's submission to her husband. It is possibly partly influenced by the custom of modest dressing in Middle Eastern cultures, but may originate more probably from the intention of keeping the bride fully covered (as a surprise?) until the actual wedding.

In Roman society the bride was dressed in white, with an orange-red veil (the *flammeum*) and a garland of flowers. In Greece the veil was yellow.

The idea of submission in the old sense has now gone from all Western wedding symbols. Both partners give themselves, it is hoped, in loving commitment, and a veil, if worn, should be seen in this light.

For no particular reason except to match the gown, white became the colour of the veil.

Something blue
This colourful tradition is still alive. It comes to us from the ancient Israelites who held that blue was the colour of purity, love, and fidelity.

The Arabs believe that blue is the colour of magical good health.

For many centuries blue was the chosen colour for the bride's garter.

Flowers
Brides used to carry orange blossoms. The orange tree blooms and reproduces in all seasons, so it is easy to understand the symbolism. The orange tree originated in China, and was brought to Europe in the Middle Ages by returning Crusaders.

Other flowers, of course, are chosen for similar meanings. The red rose was the flower dedicated to Venus, and is a symbol of love and beauty. Myrtle was favoured in centuries past as it has an enduring freshness, and meant, naturally, constancy in affection.

Bridesmaids
Some historians say these are a survival from the time of marriage by capture. They were the bride's attendants, assigned to protect her.

Flower girls
In medieval times two small girls, dressed identically, would walk before the bride in the marriage procession, carrying garlands of wheat — expressing the wish for fruitfulness and prosperity.

Bridegroom
The word itself meant a slave or servant who served or waited on the bride. Some cynics might argue that time has not changed a thing! It is worth noting, however, that this word is a symbol of the husband's submission to his wife.

Best man and groomsmen

The role of these attendants is perhaps carried over from the days of marriage by capture, when they were part of the attacking party.

In time this role was reversed. In the Middle Ages groomsmen attended the bride; and were known as the Bride's Knights. This tradition probably started earlier in the marriage-by-purchase era when men from the bride's party brought her in solemn procession to the groom's house and did not hand her over until the terms of the contract had been fulfilled.

Procession of the bride

In marriages in both ancient Rome and ancient Greece there were three basic steps:

- the *traditio puellae* — the handing over of the bride, or the giving away of the bride took place in the bride's home
- the *domum ductio* — the solemn procession of the bride to her new husband's home
- the *telos* or *confarreatio* — the uniting of the bride with the husband at his home (see also *Wedding cake*).

It is interesting to reflect that with home marriages this most ancient custom has been restored. I have officiated at marriages where it has been a most 'solemn procession' — a horse and cart, a coach and four, vintage cars, a simple red Mercedes-Benz, to say nothing, of course, of a Volkswagen or an FJ Holden!

Wedding at home

It is quite in keeping with the Roman and Greek origins of our culture to have the wedding at the home of the groom.

Music and dance

The playing of music has been part of wedding festivities for thousands of years. In many cultures (e.g. Jewish weddings), dance is also integral to the celebration.

In the wedding ceremony as most of us have inherited it (in the Anglo-Saxon style) there are no fixed traditions or rules. 'Here Comes the Bride' by Wagner, which is very firmly established as a favourite bridal entrance chorus, may be inappropriate in certain contexts.

The best music is that which is most meaningful to the bride and groom. It can be recorded, or played on any instrument. It is best played before the ceremony as the bride enters, and/or during the signing of the papers, and afterwards.

Music should be well planned and well orchestrated. The words of the chosen song must be suitable.

Words, words, words — expression of beliefs, thoughts and feelings

Fundamentally we communicate and express our feelings through the spoken word. Words are symbols — the most basic and important of all symbols.

This book is mostly about the words chosen to express the commitment, the ideals and hopes that surround it. On our own behalf and for our society we express, transmit and reinforce basic truths and values of relationships. We draw on our best poets and writers to put into words what we feel and want to say.

Marriage certificate/Signing the register

In ancient Babylonia and Assyria marriage contracts were written on clay tablets. They were included in the large collections (25,000 tablets) of Assurbanipal II of Nineveh, the world's first librarian. Archaeologists, from the time of Austin Layard and Hormuzd Rassam, have taken these tablets to the Louvre, the British Museum, and elsewhere.

The marriage tablets (the *tabulae nuptiales*) came into use in Western society for the first time during the period of the Roman emperors.

After the celebration, when the bride had been ushered into the bridal chamber and the marriage was presumed to be successfully consummated, one of two things usually happened. A sacrifice was offered to the gods, or the marriage was recorded in a register!

Throwing rice or confetti

Throwing rice or some similar cereal goes back to very ancient times. Rice, wheat and corn have always been symbolic of fertility. The ancient Greeks used to pour flour and sweets over the bridal couple, while people in Mediterranean countries used small fruits and nuts. In some countries this custom was believed also to propitiate the evil spirits.

Confetti, presumably a development of this tradition, has now become unpopular in most wedding venues for obvious reasons. There is nothing quite like rose petals, as they leave no stain, have symbolic overtones, and are easily cleaned up.

The wedding feast

Since earliest times, in every culture, all important events have been celebrated with a feast.

Wedding feasts are on record in Greece from the sixth century BC. During this meal everyone present was adorned with a garland of myrtle leaves.

The wedding cake

Eating from the same dish or drinking from the same cup is considered a binding act in many cultures, and is part of many wedding ceremonies. The common bond that unites everyone in the drinking of toasts is based on the same symbolism. The breaking of the dish or goblet was intended to drive away evil spirits.

Of all the symbols of our culture the wedding cake is the oldest; it comes from an old Roman custom:

> The bride was led to the household altar, the sacred hearth ... where she was permitted to touch the sacred fire ... Finally, the ceremony which gave its name to the entire sacral marriage service took place, the *conferreatio*. The bride and bridgroom partook of the wedding cake, the *far* or *panis farreus*, a loaf made of flour which was the 'very holy pledge of marriage'. By this act the bride and groom entered into religious communion with each other through communion with the household gods.
>
> (Schillebeeckx, p. 6).

The household gods dwelt in the hearth fire of the Roman house, and this fire was never allowed to go out. The wedding cake was cooked over this fire in the groom's house, and the bride, once she ate some of the cake, became, through the life of the gods of that family, part of the household of her husband.

This is one reason the groom carried the bride over the threshold — so that she would not touch the house until she was officially part of it.

Giving of gifts

A very natural symbol of the expression of love, and the desire to gain favour. Among the American Indians, for example, gifts were given by the brave to the fair maiden's father. If the father accepted the gift, the betrothal was sealed.

In other cultures the interchange of gifts actually constituted the wedding ceremony.

Throwing the bouquet

In early fourteenth-century France it was considered a lucky omen to secure the bride's blue garter. There was a general rush for it at the conclusion of the wedding ceremony, and many were injured or roughed up in the scramble.

This developed into the practice of the bride throwing her stocking away. It eventually became easier to throw the bouquet instead.

The belief grew that the lucky lady who caught the bouquet would be the next to marry, so the custom passed from an enthusiastic scramble by males to an enthusiastic jump by females.

Honeymoon

The 'honey' part of the word originates from the custom of drinking mead — a wine made from honey — for a month ('moon') after the wedding.

In the time of marriage by capture, the bride and bridegroom went into hiding for a period until the hue and cry had died down.

In our legal code and in Christian belief the definition is that a marriage is not truly so until it has been consummated (that sexual intercourse has taken place).

In some cultures evidence of the bride's defloration, as seen by stains on the sheets of the bridal bed, was often necessary before the marriage was accepted as such.

The Bulgarians used to lock their newly-weds together for a week; the marsh Arabs of Iraq would put the couple in a tent, give the groom a gun, and instruct him to fire it once consummation has taken place! The wedding party, some distance away, could then start the celebrations.

Anniversaries

Many wedding anniversaries are celebrated in Western culture. Most do not call for a ceremony, but some do — for silver, golden and diamond wedding anniversaries.

At times a married couple may feel it is appropriate to express and renew their love and commitment. Such ceremonies are full of warmth and feeling.

The anniversaries (and gifts, when appropriate) are generally classified as follows:

1st	Cotton or paper	30th	Pearl or ivory
3rd	Leather	35th	Jade or coral
5th	Wood	40th	Ruby
10th	Tin	45th	Sapphire
12th	Linen and silk	**50th**	**Golden**
15th	Crystal	55th	Emerald
20th	China	**60th**	**Diamond**
25th	**Silver**		

Part 2

OTHER CEREMONIES

5 The Need for Other Ceremonies

Celebrants now understand that a wide range of ceremonies are necessary to fill human need, benefit society, and add meaning and purpose to people's lives.

It does not take much reflection to realise that our lives are full of ritual and ceremony. At the Melbourne Cricket Ground, near where I live, patrons attend at certain times, wear special clothes, chant special songs with extraordinary enthusiasm, engage in fellow-feeling and traditional banter, eat the sacred food and drink — pie, tomato sauce and beer — all centred on a spectacle that is full of hope, feeling and fervour.

The same people probably have a ritual caffeine fix at the same time every day, have a candlelit dinner with husband/wife/lover at certain days of the year, and cannibalise the Easter Bunny in a 'death by chocolate' routine that makes no sense to anyone except it is what you do on that occasion. It is ritual. It is tradition.

On the more serious side, we all know men or women who grieve bitterly for years over a divorce, and who, we suspect, never get over it, because the marriage never really ended in a definite way. There is no 'closure', as we say. There was nothing to trigger off a healthy grief process — no event to make the person live through it and get on with life. Melbourne celebrant Beryl Shaw has now officiated at over 200 divorce ceremonies with marvellous beneficial effect.

There is, in my opinion, a major problem in our society in defining the relationship between stepparents and stepchildren. On the few occasions I have written role and acceptance rituals for steprelations into a marriage ceremony, my reports are that the effects have been excellent.

My colleague, Ted Logan, met a lady who hated her given name and wanted to change it. Now how do you do that? In a ceremony, of course. So Ted devised a ceremony, all her friends were invited, the first given name was duly expunged and another brought in to replace it. The message was clear, and the ceremony had the desired effect. The best way to do these things is through ceremony.

In civil naming ceremonies, which we effectively restarted throughout the world, celebrants take great satisfaction in establishing, defining and expounding the principles of the relationship between godparent and godchild. What a wonderful thing for a child to have additional protectors and loved ones! We do this in a ceremony, and I am convinced that the better the ceremony the more deeply the relationship is taken on board.

Joseph Campbell, a famous American anthropologist, believes that the level of civilisation in a society is directly proportional to the number of ceremonies practised in that society.

I personally believe that there is a desperate need in our society for a 'secular bar mitzvah', 'an introduction to adolescence', as some people like to call it. My colleagues, Mary Hancock (in New Zealand) and Lyn Knorr, have developed such a ceremony, but it is not yet happening on a wide scale. Teachers and youth workers say that young people feel alienated, that they suffer from 'disconnectedness'. How could you feel alienated and disconnected if all your family and your friends and your teachers gathered round you and told you, in a ceremony, that they understand you are having a struggle, that they love you, that they support you, that they esteem you, that they are interested in you, that you have a network of encouragement, that you have them to call on. They tell you this in words and gestures, and poetry and symbol and song — and here are some gifts and a party to nail it down. How could you feel disconnected after that? If you were a 14-year-old, would you go from that to smash phone boxes and paint graffiti on the nearest wall? I think not. Joseph Campbell is right.

In 1973 celebrants started by officiating at weddings. The first challenge was to improve the weddings. Then came namings. We had to invent a naming ceremony, and we have now improved on it. After that came funerals; we didn't like that challenge much, but we knew we had to do it, and do it well.

Then we realised that there were bigger dimensions to this role than we had ever thought of. We realised that we had a responsibility to encourage the arts and the culture, to strengthen relationships, to fill a psychological and spiritual gap — a result of the decline in church attendances. We also had a role to transmit and reinforce values, to reinforce good conventions of behaviour and morality.

Now we see that different people need different strengthening occasions at varying times in their lives. Some seem to need them more than others. The broad spectrum of ceremonies now challenges all civil celebrants. Here is a list.

FLAGSHIP CEREMONIES

Wedding
Namegiving
Funeral

SOME OTHER CEREMONIES

Secular bar mitzvah/adolescence
Coming of age
Renewal of vows
Divorce

Stepparent/stepchildren acceptance
Change of name
Menopause
Retirement/redundancy
House dedication
Commencing a new business
Change of business premises
Creating a special place
30th, 40th, 50th, 60th, ..., birthdays
Cycles of seven/special birthdays
Naturalisation/citizenship (public or private)
Graduation (public or private)

PUBLIC CEREMONIES

National tragedy/grief
National celebration

SEASONAL CEREMONIES

Vernal equinox
Autumnal equinox
Summer solstice
Winter solstice
Seasons
Cultural traditions

To create a personalised ceremony of a challenging kind, a great deal of 'process' is needed, and it is very time consuming. Be prepared to negotiate a reasonable fee with the celebrant.

There is insufficient space to include an example of every kind of ceremony, but information is available on these ceremonies from the Australian Federation of Civil Celebrants Inc., and the Federation will be pleased to put you in touch with a professional celebrant dedicated to quality and excellence in ceremonies.

---

*In all ceremonies substitute your own names and the names of the other people involved for the names in italics.

6 Namegiving/Naming

Namegiving ceremonies have a history almost as old as the human race. Any who have seen the classic film Ben Hur will recall how, when Ben Hur saved the Roman general, the latter named him as his son. A son was not a legal member of the family until the father had named him in a ceremony. Thus a full legal son of the family, in our terms, could be adopted, born out of wedlock, born of the wife or of another woman. Naming (or namegiving) was the rite that brought the child into the family.

Namegiving ceremonies, as celebrants now do them, however, are relatively new. Ever since some celebrants in the mid 1970s started to officiate at them, they have become increasingly popular.

A namegiving ceremony is not a baptism or a christening, though it is sometimes referred to as a 'secular christening'. Such ceremonies are by definition religious, and do not come within the scope of this book.

The namegiving ceremony conducted by a civil celebrant is a fulfilling and meaningful experience for all concerned. It is an occasion when a new birth is celebrated and a child welcomed into the world. Family relationships are deepened, and the parents become more fully aware of their responsibilities.

So, of course, do the godparents (I can see nothing wrong with using this word in its cultural sense, although some celebrants prefer 'mentors' or 'guardians').

So, too, do the grandparents — their inclusion and recognition in the ceremony is an initiative of celebrants. The naming ceremony also has a community dimension, represented by the wider circle of family and friends.

The naming ceremony is an excellent occasion for the cultural expression of joy, hope and acceptance, and should in time draw forth the best of our music and literature. Many religious people are now choosing the non-religious naming service to celebrate the birth of their child. Many Christians, for example, do not believe in infant baptism, so choose this cultural celebration and leave the child free to choose or not to choose baptism in the late teens. In fact, all naming ceremonies are done or performed on this principle.

The namegiving ceremony also responds to the cultural and community need to welcome a child into the family and the world, to remind all concerned of the great responsibility involved in bringing up a child, and to recognise and appoint those who will have an important role in the child's development. Certificates for parents, godparents, grandparents and great-grandparents are issued to record the event.

The ceremony does have some legal significance: a naming certificate signed by five witnesses (i.e. celebrant, parents, godparents) would be accepted by the courts as sufficient evidence to rectify a 'non-record of birth' situation (when a birth is not registered with state authorities due to mistake or negligence) or to rectify a wrongful entry in the records. I look forward to the day when the naming ceremony becomes the occasion when the name and the birth are registered (in the same way the celebrant registers the marriage).

Of all the ceremonies celebrants conduct, namegivings are the most difficult. This is because there is usually a number of children present to distract everyone. The baby in question can take the attention in various ways by crying, laughing, or goo-gooing, and the celebrant may end up talking to no one. To counteract this and retain some atmosphere, I usually tell people in the beginning how difficult it is to officiate at such ceremonies, how distractions easily occur, and how if some of them, at least, pay attention to the words, the ceremony will be much more meaningful. This little appeal is usually successful!

Note that:

* the words must reflect the values of the parents and the family, and the celebrant must be comfortable about the words said
* the ending is most important — the final words must leave everyone on a 'high'
* the ceremony should be, as it were, a story, a story that unfolds
* the introduction is greatly enhanced if it contains personal details, obtained by personal interview
* the godparents will help the parents mould the child's future. As godparenting is a great honour, the godparents should feel their happiness, as well as their responsibilities. Some celebrants should speak to the godparents before the ceremony, in the presence of the parents, and tell them that their commitment is ongoing, and then, using the godparents' full names, ask them pledge their guidance and affection publicly.

A kiss for the child after the pledge is a symbol of the bond.

Naming Ceremony

INTRODUCTION [NI 1]

Celebrant: Friends,

We meet here to take part, together, in a simple ceremony. We do so for a number of reasons.

Tania and *Paul* wish to express their joy to you on the birth of *Tiffany*. They are pleased that she has arrived safely in this world. They want to welcome her into their family unit, to the wider family of their relatives, and to the community of their friends and the world. They wish you all to share this joy. (Personal observations may be inserted here.)

Mixed with the happiness that *Tania* and *Paul* have is also a certain awe at the immense responsibility that is now theirs. This welcome to little *Tiffany* will remind them that from now on a great deal of their lives will be involved in caring for her, guiding her development, and nurturing her growth as a human being. Just as they wish you to share their joy, they also ask you to share their responsibility.

It is certain that the more love this child receives, the more she will benefit in her life, and the more love in turn she will be able to give to others. The more people to whom this child relates, the more balanced and rich her growth will be.

So your presence at this celebration today is appreciated, as will be your interest and involvement in the years ahead.

READINGS

We reflect on the potential of this child, and on the wonderful possibilities that lie before her.

Adapted from A Recipe for Dreaming [NR 1]

Nature formed you with perfect feet and hands and a heart that beats non-stop, sometimes for a hundred years. You were made complete.

You have inherited a thousand generations of wisdom, skill, poetry, song, all the sunrises and sunsets of knowledge past. You are the sum of all the people who went before you.

You are a refinery of all inherited intellectual wealth, the full flood of antecedent wisdom is piped and stored within you — how to climb the highest mountain, slay the biggest monster, how to survive fear and how to summon your own courage and take pride in your wonderful intelligence.

Inside you are more possibilities than you could possibly use up in one lifetime.

If you can dream it, you can do it, because the instinctive knowledge of how to succeed is already programmed within you waiting to be turned on, it is waiting to flow like a river as you come on stream.

Bryce Courtenay

Celebrant: This celebration also is an occasion when *Tania* and *Paul* want to make themselves aware of their proper role as parents. This, they feel, is expressed well in these words:

From The Prophet   [NR 2]

Your children are not your children.
They are the sons and daughters of Life's longing for itself.
They come through you but not from you.
And though they are with you yet they belong not to you.
You may give them your love but not your thoughts, for they have their own thoughts.
You may house their bodies but not their souls, for their souls dwell in the house of tomorrow, which you can not visit, not even in your dreams.
You may strive to be like them, but seek not to make them like you, for life goes not backward nor tarries with yesterday.
You are the bows from which your children as living arrows are sent forth.

Kahlil Gibran

Celebrant: The next reading involves us all. As a community of friends and family, we all share a responsibility to provide the atmosphere in which young Tiffany will develop as a person.

A Child Learns What She Lives   [NR 3]

If a child lives with criticism,
    she learns to condemn.
If a child lives with hostility,
    she learns to fight.
If a child lives with ridicule,
    she learns to be shy.

If a child lives with shame,
    she learns to feel guilt.

But,
If a child lives with tolerance,
    she learns to be patient.
If a child lives with encouragement,
    she learns confidence.
If a child lives with fairness,
    she learns justice.
If a child lives with security,
    she learns to have faith.
If a child lives with approval,
    she learns to like herself.
If a child lives with acceptance and friendship,
    she learns to find love in the world.

Traditional

GRANDPARENTS [NG 1]

Celebrant: It is not always possible for grandparents to involve themselves in the development of their grandchildren, but when they do it is a great bonus and blessing. The important role played by grandparents is the passing on of cultural values to children.

They assist children find their identity and their inner security, and to integrate themselves into society. The special relationship of trust and mutual enjoyment that develops between child and grandparent is something very special. Through this relationship children learn their lineage, their history, and many values and skills.

This cultural inheritance lays the foundation for young people to construct their personality during childhood and adolescence, and adds great meaning to their existence.

For this reason *Tania* and *Paul* wish to recognise and express their gratitude that *Tiffany*'s grandparents, *John* and *Kathy*, and *Daniel* and *Sally*, are here today.

WISHES FOR THE CHILD [NW 1]

Guests queue up, and, one by one, in ritual manner, read one of the following wishes, or one they have composed themselves.

First Guest: *Melanie,*
On behalf of everyone present, and on my own behalf, I wish you (these words begin each wish) — long life and great happiness.

The ritual is repeated with the following wishes, usually read from prepared cards.
* good health and a head full of hair
* the enjoyment of many pleasures
* a peaceful world to live in
* true friends and satisfying relationships
* a healed and healthy environment
* a creative spirit
* a curious and inquisitive mind
* a sense of wonder
* an appreciation of your roots and your cultural heritage from Canada (or wherever), from Australia, from your world, that never leaves you
* a true social conscience
* a full life of passion and enthusiasm
* an awareness that you are a citizen of the world
* inner security and a sense of self-worth
* an appreciation of Australian Rules football (or whatever), and even some of the other sports!

MENTORS OR GODPARENTS [NV 1]

Celebrant: An important tradition on these occasions is the responsibility accepted by mentors or godparents.

In this age of the nuclear family, when many of us live to a great extent isolated from our family and friends, godparents have perhaps an even more important role today than they have had in the past.

They undertake a special and lifelong interest in the welfare of their godchild, and assume a more-than-ordinary responsibility in the event of the death or default of the parents. (The personal qualities of the godparents can be mentioned briefly as the reason they were chosen by the parents.)

I now ask the godparents: Are you, *Michael* and *Julia*, willing to accept this important responsibility?

Godparents: We are.

Celebrant: *Julia* and *Michael*,
Will you stay close to *Tiffany*?
To the best of your ability,
will you guide her through life
so that she may know the best way you know?
Will you touch her with your wisdom?
Will you try to be a good influence
by your own way of living,
and encourage her to observe
worthy principles of living,
and decent treatment of her fellow-human beings
and her world?

Godparents: We will.

Celebrant: Then, with me, touch the child.

NAMING [N 1]

Celebrant (everyone repeats, phrase by phrase):
We all agree to call you *Tiffany Louise McIntyre*,
So we therefore name you *Tiffany Louise McIntyre*.
We wish you long life and happiness,
in a loving and peaceful world.
May you bring joy to your parents,
your godparents, your grandparents,
to all of us — your family and friends.
May you be one who makes this world
a better and happier place.

Celebrant: *Tiffany*,
Your parents chose this name with love and they give it to you with love. This name they give to you to accompany you throughout your life with all the qualities of strength and goodness your name implies.

(The meaning of the name chosen, such as a grandparent's name, or the reason for the choice, can be explained here.)

FINAL DECLARATION [ND 1]

Celebrant: Friends,
This ceremony will in no way inhibit this child from seeking the truth during her life and any future commitments to religious or non-religious beliefs. In fact, it is our duty in the coming years to present to her a broad and balanced view of life, and encourage her in the virtues we all agree as good — integrity, honesty, concern, fairness and love toward others.

I conclude this ceremony by summarising the thought that has been the theme today. Let us all be aware that our lives are interrelated, that this ceremony will strengthen the affection and the friendship we all have for each other, but especially the relationship now established by each and every one of us with *Tiffany*.

Tiffany, May life's richest joys and blessings be yours. May you grow in health of body and mind to full adulthood, and may it be your good fortune to play some worthy part in making life more pleasant for those whose paths you cross.

Friends, I have the honour to present *Tiffany Louise McIntyre*. (Applause!)

PRESENTATION [NP 1]

The naming certificate and the guest list (on the naming certificate envelope), the godparent and grandparent certificates are then signed and presented.

During the presentation of the certificates the celebrant may call the presentees forward; the parents of the child can then thank them personally, and present the certificates. Sometimes godparents and grandparents may wish to respond briefly.

Some celebrants like to make a presentation to the child of a gift, perhaps a plant or similar. A plant, for example, could be presented using the words: 'A child, not unlike a plant, given the right amount of light and shade, well-tended soil, and nurturing in a loving environment, will grow. She will become a flower in full bloom, she will bring beauty to her world.'

The guests are invited to congratulate the parents and the godparents.

Candle-lighting Ceremonies

(Celebrant: Kathleen Hurley)
Candles are used in ceremonies to symbolise and express cultural and social values. With the namegiving ceremony, a namegiving candle can be lit for the child.

SHONA [NC 1]

Celebrant: Ladies and Gentlemen,
I begin this ceremony for *Shona* today by playing a beautiful song *Ellie* and *Shayne* have chosen for their daughter.

During this time they will light *Shona's* namegiving candle. I invite the grandparents, great-grandparents and godparents to come forward to light their candles too.

AMY [NC 2]

Celebrant: I now ask *Andrew* and *Pia* to light and hold the candle.

The lighting of the candle is a ceremonial acknowledgement by the godparents/mentors that they accept the responsibilities associated with mentoring. The flame of the candle represents the light that will guide and protect *Amy* through life's journey of tears and laughter, of joy and sorrow, and of happiness and sadness, and great love.

Each year on this child's birthday the godparents/mentors are invited to relight the candle until the child reaches eighteen. The candle will then be kept to be relit on those very special occasions that occur in the journey through life.

At the end of the ceremony, the godparents/mentors extinguish the candle, and hand it to the mother.

Namegiving Ceremony: A Single Parent

It is easy to rewrite any namegiving ceremony to make it suitable for a single parent, by changing all the references to parents to 'the mother' or 'the father'.

Writing Your Own Ceremony

As for any other cultural ceremony, you must feel that the words truly reflect your thoughts and sentiments.

Parents and family can adapt or write their own introduction, insert their own quotations, ask various members of the family to read, and so on. The following pages also give some alternative readings.

Alternatives

INTRODUCTION

JASON [NI 2]

Celebrant: Friends,

In Western culture this ceremony goes back to Roman and Greek practice in pre-Christian times. The renowned scholar, Edward Schillebeeckx, tells us that a child was not a member of the family until the celebrant had named him or her at the naming ceremony. Almost every nation in the world has the equivalent of a cultural naming ceremony.

Thus a child born out of wedlock, an adopted child, or even a child born in wedlock had no status in culture or law until the celebrant (in the days of ancient Rome, the father) had made the decision to so make the child a member of the family. Thus, ties of kinship were established.

Today we bring *Jason* into his family, we decide to bring him closer to all of us.

In this ceremony we consciously decide to bring her closer to all of us. It is our close relationship that give most meaning to our lives. Today we celebrate the coming of a child into our personal world, into a loving family, into a network of friends.

The special relationship of grandparent and grandchild will be recognised and acknowledged. We.therefore honour *Ailsa* and *Philip, Lorna* and *Rodney.*

Similarly, another of our culture's closest relationships will also be established today — that of godparent. I use this word in the cultural and human sense, not in any religious sense. The godparents, *Rachel* and *Troy*, traditionally undertake a special and lifelong interest in the welfare of their godchild, and to assume a more-than-ordinary responsibility in the event of the death or default of the parents.

Another decision has been made today: *Robert* and *Brigid*, the parents of *Jason*, have invited you today because they recognise you as family and close friends — those whom they want to be associated with their child.

FIONA [NI 3]

(Celebrant, Kathleen Hurley)

Celebrant: A baby is a traveller in time. From fragments of yourselves you have created someone utterly new and unlike any other.

Your child is someone who sets off on a first journey. You can only accompany her a little, for she is bound for a time you will not see, springs and summers beyond your knowing.

Your child is so small, so dependent upon your care, yet she is a summary of all the centuries that have passed since the world began.

She holds the key to all knowledge that has been harvested, to all speculation; and she is filled with the old insatiable desire to learn.

Your child lies quiet in your arms, yet carries the seeds of creation, humans' obsessive need to make cathedrals and bread, bridges and laws, and hundred-metre murals.

She is your own dearly loved child, yet every second takes her further from you. She wants so little — warmth, food and love — but seeks them with an urgency and determination out of all proportion to her tiny body.

Do not love your child as a possession or she will break your heart. She is already beyond your understanding; and yet, something of her will always need those first things — warmth, food and love. As you fill her basic needs she is already learning how to give and receive — the first elements of what you will teach her.

NAMING [N 2]

The parents (repeating the following words after the celebrant):

> We love you, and we proudly name you *Domenica Caldwell McKenzie*.
> We will all call you *Domenica Caldwell McKenzie*.
> We wish for you long life and happiness in a loving and peaceful world.

GRANDPARENTS' BLESSING [NG 2]

First grandmother:

> I, *Ethel*, your grandmother, represent the East.
> Welcome, dear *Euridice*.
> Join us here as the butterfly in flight.
> I evoke the gentle breeze of spring and the soft scent of flowers.
> May it be a part of every breath and every word spoken by you and to you.

First grandfather:

> I, *Kenneth*, your grandfather, represent the South.
> Welcome, dear *Euridice*.
> Join us here as the hearth fire.
> I evoke the warmth and the brightness of the summer's sun.
> May this warmth and sunlight be a part of every song you hear,
> and every loving embrace you ever receive.

Second grandfather:

I, *James*, your grandfather, represent the West.

Welcome, dear *Euridice*.

Join us here as the babbling brook, ever searching, ever singing.

As the rain falls to give new life to the earth below may all life's bounty sustain you.

May you share this bounty with others in love and joy.

Second grandmother:

I, *Faye*, your grandmother, represent the North.

Welcome, dear *Euridice*.

Join us as the trees stand against the sky.

May you stand strong.

May you walk in strength and confidence.

May you keep your feet on the ground, but always reach for the stars.

GUARDIANS/GODPARENTS/MENTORS

THOMAS [NV 2]
(Celebrant, Joyce Edmonds)

Celebrant: Guardians and godparents are very special people who are always available to help guide and give support, and to offer loyalty and love, and to be an example to those under their care.

Dougal and *Sophie* have asked *Alison* and *Gareth* to be appointed as the guardians for their son, *Thomas*, and to stand together with them in the responsibilities they have accepted today.

Alison, as the guardian of *Thomas*, will you pledge your loyalty, love and support to *Sophie* and *Dougal* in the rearing of this very special and loved child?

Alison: I do.

Celebrant: *Gareth*, as the guardian of *Thomas*, will you accept the responsibility that is offered to you today by Dougal and Sophie in the life of Thomas?

Gareth: I do.

Celebrant: On behalf of *Dougal* and *Sophie*, I present you with these guardian certificates, signifying your willingness and acceptance of this role.

READINGS

(Many readings, like this one, can easily be adapted for a boy or a girl.)

Little One [NR 4]

Bless this little heart, this white soul that has won the kiss
of heaven for our earth.
She loves the light of the sun, she loves the sight of her
mother's face.
She has not learned to despise the dust, nor to hanker
after gold.
Clasp her to your heart and bless her.
She has come into this land of one hundred crossroads;
I know not how she chose you from the crowd, how
she came to your door, and grasped your hand to ask
you the way.
She will follow you, laughing and talking and not a
doubt in her heart.
Keep her trust, lead her straight and bless her.
Lay your hand on her head, and pray that, though the
waves underneath grow threatening, yet the breath
from above may come and fill her sails and waft her
to the haven of peace.
Forget her not in your hurry, let her come to your heart,
and bless her.

Rabindranath Tagore

Adapted from To My Mother [NR 5]

'Where have I come from,
where did you pick me up?'
the baby asked its mother.

She answered, half-crying, half-laughing,
and clasped the baby to her breast,
'You were hidden in my heart as its desire, my
    darling.
You were in the dolls of my childhood's games;
in all my hopes and my loves, in my life,
in the life of my mother you have lived.

When in girlhood my heart was opening its petals,
You hovered as a fragrance about it.
Your tender softness bloomed in my youthful limbs,
like a glow in the sky before sunrise.

Heaven's first darling,
twin-born with the morning light,
you have floated down the stream of the world's life,
and at last you have arrived in my heart.

As I gaze on your face, mystery overwhelms me;
you who belong to all have become mine.
For fear of losing you I hold you tight to my breast.
What magic has snared the world's treasure in my
    arms?'

Rabindranath Tagore

Dads and Daughters [NR 6]

Each love in life is precious
With a meaning all its own,
Like the bond of Dad to daughter,
And a strength of love that's grown.

He's there in times of trouble,
And when she needs a special friend,
He's the figure she relies on,
And on whom she can depend.

She gives to him that something
Only fathers can portray,
Of a love so pure and endless,
And of joy in every way.

From the first steps ever taken,
To her walking down the aisle,
He views her with unending pride,
And a love that makes him smile.

Dads are very special
And no one ever takes their place,
Though many loves can come and go,
They'll always have that cherished space.

Liana Preston

May Your Wishes All Come True   [NR 7]

May you always do for others
And let others do for you,
May you build a ladder to the stars
And climb on every rung,
And may you stay forever young.

May you grow up to be righteous,
May you grow up to be true,
May you always know the truth
And see the light surrounding you,
May you always be courageous,
Stand upright and be strong,
And may you stay forever young.

May your hands always be busy
And may your feet always be swift,
May you have a strong foundation
When the winds of changes shift,
May your heart always be joyful
May your song always be sung,
And may you stay forever young.

A Parent's Wish   [NR 8]

I'd really like for you to know about hand-me-down
    clothes and homemade icecream and leftover
    meat loaf.

I hope you learn humility by being humiliated.

I hope you learn honesty by being cheated.

I hope you learn to make your own bed, mow the lawns, wash the car.

I hope nobody gives you a brand-new car when you're seventeen.

I hope you have a job by then.

It will be good at least one time for you to see a baby lamb born, or your old dog put to sleep.

I hope you get a black eye fighting for something you believe in.

I hope you have to share a bedroom with your younger brother — by the way it's all right to draw a line down the middle of the room!

When he wants to crawl under the covers with you because he's scared, I hope you let him.

I hope you have to walk uphill to school with your friend, and I hope you live in a town where you can do it safely.

I hope you learn to dig in the dirt.

I hope you learn to play marbles and read books, and I hope when you learn those newfangled computers you also learn how to add up and subtract in your bright little mind.

I hope your friends give you a bad time when you have your first girlfriend, and I hope when you talk back to your mother you'll learn the taste of soap,

and I hope you skin your knee climbing mountains.

May you feel sorrow at a funeral, and may you feel absolute happiness on your birthday.

I hope your mother punishes you when you throw a cricket ball through a neighbour's window,

and I hope she hugs and kisses you at Christmas time when you buy her a bottle of the worst perfume money can buy.

These things I wish for you: tough times and disappointment, hard work and happiness.

7 Milestone Celebrations

- Teenage rites of passage
- Coming of age
- Special birthdays

Ceremony at Adolescence (13th Birthday), or Second Cycle of Seven (14th Birthday)

Perhaps the most needed ceremony in our developing culture, for non-churchgoers, is the adolescence (becoming a young adult) ceremony, the secular bar mitzvah, the civil confirmation. It can be held for the thirteenth birthday (the entry to the teenage years), the fourteenth birthday (the second cycle of seven), or at any time deemed appropriate.

By way of introduction I quote from a speech at such a ceremony given by the pioneering New Zealand celebrant, Mary Hancock.

> No matter what ceremony I am designing and celebrating, I am always mindful of the three key stages that make up the core of the process of the ceremony or ritual. These

were first developed by Arnold Van Gennep in 1908, and are as appropriate today as they were ninety years ago.

Adolescence can be one of the most turbulent times in our human journey of growth and development. The use of ceremony and ritual can be of great assistance in marking this major transition. It can affirm the importance of the adolescents, and honour the changes that they will undergo in this cocoon stage, emerging, like butterflies, in adulthood. As Juliet Batten commented, 'We need rituals at many times — whether for healing or transition, celebration or mourning. To learn to create our own is to empower ourselves, and this can enrich our lives immeasurably.'

- The first stage of a ceremony is the beginning, which is about separating and letting go.
- The second stage is the major part of the ceremony: the threshold, the manifestation. The actual transition takes place here.
- The final stage is reintegration – the new place from which ordinary life is resumed. Everything is brought together at this point, and a new status is acknowledged and affirmed.

Beginning of separation

Before the ceremony the adolescent is invited to collect a large box of symbols of all the things of childhood that he or she is now ready to leave behind (such as toys, teddies, clothes, games, etc.), and another box of symbols of things to take into adolescence (skateboard, schoolbag, Walkman, CDs, tapes, clothes, etc.).

Give at least a week to think about this, and to select the symbols. The parents should be open to talking with the teenager during this selection, as it is quite a big thing to do, and can have a huge impact as the young person reflects and makes these conscious choices.

The ceremony

After welcoming the family and friends the celebrant gives an introduction to the ceremony, explaining the reason for it.

Then the formal part of the ceremony begins. The celebrant invites the young person to come forward and place the box of symbols of childhood in front, and to explain the move to a new stage in life (adolescence) and the leaving of that part of life (childhood) behind.

The teenager is invited to take the other box of symbols (those to be taken forward into adolescence) and to place it at the other side of the room. The young person is then asked to stand beside the childhood box until ready to cross the room to sit down next to the adolescent box.

The celebrant then welcomes all to the ceremony, and begins by recounting from one of the many works of literature a story of adolescent journeying.

Threshold and manifestation

The celebrant invites the young person, accompanied by the family and friends, to come outside, emphasising that this is like a new space — this is the beginning of the adolescent space. The teenager is then given time to gather wood and make a fire, taking as long as wished to build the fire, and to throw on as little or as much wood as wanted. Some young people may decide to stand, reflect and feed wood onto it; others to put it out in some way.

For many young people this is quite an awesome event, as they may never have had the full responsibility before for lighting and maintaining a fire.

This fire is symbolic of the transitions in adolescence.

Wishes and wisdom

When the fire has died down, the family and friends honour this young person by each telling a short story or passing on some wisdom, or giving a wish or blessing — a special honouring as they make this transition at adolescence, the beginning of the journey towards adulthood.

Reintegration

At the completion of these affirmations by family and friends, the celebrant formally invites the young person to come back into the family's house, to be welcomed by the parents (or close family and friends), and given a gift as a symbol of adolescence.

The ceremony is closed with a wish for a safe and exciting journey through adolescence for the teenager, and the festivities begin.

13th Birthday Ceremony

This adolescence (becoming a teenager) ceremony was prepared and conducted by Lyn Knorr (who enjoys the distinction of being the second civil celebrant appointed in Australia), and is reproduced with the permission of Lucia and Daniel Blums.

Celebrant: As special people for Daniel Blums, you are warmly welcomed to celebrate this special birthday, his thirteenth, the beginning of his teenage years.

Why a ceremony? you might ask. Well, a ceremony allows us to stand still, to focus on the important matter at hand, to consider Dan's life and all that he means to us, to express our wishes and hopes for his future, to celebrate this special birthday, to acknowledge what is significant at this stage in his life.

Your presence at this celebration today is appreciated, as will be your interest and involvement in the years ahead. What we can be certain of is that the more love Daniel receives, the more love in turn he will be able to give to others. The more people to whom he relates, the more balanced and rich his life will be.

These few words cannot encompass all that Daniel means to his parents, Lucia and Rudy, his brother Christopher, his grandparents, Anna and Sam and Marta, his godfather Raff, his godmother Joanne, and to all of you, his relatives and friends. But they can emphasise those things that will make us a memory, a special time that we can share, an occasion when we can, together, wish Dan a good and happy life.

This is a significant stage in his life. He leaves childhood behind, and moves on to adolescence, that transitional period to adulthood. The work of adolescence is not easy. As in childhood each step requires new tasks of development, but demands the letting go of techniques that worked before.

With each step some magic must be given up, some old safe way of doing things must go to allow for the expansion of Dan's own distinctiveness. This new stage prepares his way to adulthood and there will be many challenges for him in the coming years — emotionally, spiritually, intellectually and physically, but there will also be many rewards. There are exciting times ahead with lots of new things to learn and experience.

But you won't be alone, Dan. To make the task easier we hope you will learn from your parents their best traits, and that you will confirm for yourself the values shown by their example. We hope that they will give you the freedom to find your own way, that they will stand beside you when you need them, and stand aside when it is time for you to seek your personal destiny; in this way passing on to you the concept of family as a transcendent force that brings people close in time of joy and in time of need.

We hope that your home continues to provide you with an island of sanity and peace — a home with books and poetry and music, a home that encompasses the beauty of nature, that has within it the elements of humour and joy, and a harmony with the rhythms of life, a home that represents the highest strivings of men and woman.

READINGS

Celebrant: Daniel, your mother would like to pass on to you some advice. (Daniel's mother, Lucia, then read in full from *The Desiderata*, and an extract from *A Recipe for Dreaming* by Bryce Courtney (see NR1)).

WISHES

Celebrant: We now come to that part of the ceremony where you, Daniel's family and friends, all get the opportunity to express your wishes for him. (See the previous ceremony.)

While Christopher is handing out the wishes, we will hear a most appropriate song that Rudy found for Dan, about a boy in a flour-sack cape — who did not know he could not fly, so he did! (Everyone is supplied with the words of the song so that they can follow it easily while it is being played.)

Celebrant: Would you now please each read your wishes aloud, and as you do so, pass them to Dan?

Wishes of one or two words, up to a paragraph (for example, for health, prosperity, long life), can be written on card, and handed to Dan. For the style of the wishes that could be used see p. 98.

Celebrant: Dan, now is the opportunity for you to respond.

Daniel makes a short speech of thanks.

Celebrant: Daniel,
> We wish you a fulfilling and happy life in a home full of love and truth.
> May you grow up to reflect the best of your mother and father, and to extend to all your relationships the love you have received from them.

Please all join me in singing happy birthday to Dan.

Coming of Age (traditionally at 21, often now at 18)

Youth is like spring, an overpraised season.
— *Samuel Butler*

It is deeply embedded in the customs of most cultures that society requires a ceremony to mark the transition from youth to adulthood.

Is eighteen or twenty-one the correct age to celebrate the transition to full adulthood? Why not nineteen or twenty? I heard a person on talkback radio passionately claiming that one is not an adult until one is twenty-four! Is the key to the door still an appropriate symbol? How does the right to vote, to get married, to die for one's country, to drink in hotels, to drive a car, to finish high school, come into all of this? What multicultural symbols and values should we profitably assimilate?

Coming of age used to be celebrated on the twenty-first birthday, but a ceremony is now common on the eighteenth birthday (and some people celebrate both!).

The traditional ceremony went something like this:

- Father's speech to son or daughter — sometimes deepened by an appropriate poem. Other speeches by the mother, best friend, or others, are optional.
- Presentation by father of the symbolic key to the door.
- Reply by the daughter or son.
- Cutting of the cake.
- Proposal of a toast by a family member or friend (optional).
- Singing of songs: 'Happy Birthday', etc.
- Three cheers.

This ceremony needs a great deal more development in the light of principles espoused elsewhere in this book. The time has come for a much more structured ceremony.

21st Birthday Ceremony

(Celebrant, Mary Hancock)

For *Alani*'s ceremony everyone sat in a large circle on cushions, amidst a huge and splendid array of spring flowers.

WELCOME AND INTRODUCTION

Celebrant: I am Mary Hancock, a celebrant.

We are here today to honour and celebrate with *Alani*, as she moves through a major 'rite of passage' to adulthood on her twenty-first birthday. Please join us in this ritual.

READING

From The Heroine in Every Woman   [MCR 1]

There is a potential heroine in every woman. She is the leading lady in her own life story, on a journey that begins at her birth and continues through her lifetime. As she travels on her particular path, she will undoubtedly encounter suffering; feel loneliness, vulnerability, uncertainty, and know limitations. She may also find meaning, develop character, experience love and grace, and learn wisdom. To be a heroine on her own heroic journey, a woman must begin with the attitude that her choices do matter. In this process of living from this premise, something happens; a woman becomes a choicemaker, a heroine who shapes who she will become. She either grows or is diminished by what she does or does not do and by the attitudes she holds.

Jean Bollen

Celebrant: In her heroic journey *Alani* is already honouring the choicemaker — her desire for a ritual at her twenty-first birthday, to make a major transition in her life, to honour herself and her journey.

WEB OF CONNECTIONS

Celebrant: I invite you now to take time to weave a web of connections between ourselves and *Alani*. Take time to share, to spin, to weave connections and reminiscences of your relationship to her. To do this, we will pass a special speaking shell from Vanuatu (*Alani*'s longtime home) to hold as each of us talks and shares. *Kawena*, *Alani*'s mother, will begin.

Each person talks and shares.

MEDITATION/QUIET REFLECTION

Celebrant: We have space and time now for a gentle reflective meditation for *Alani*. Take time to think of *Alani*, reflecting on all the interconnections we have spun and woven together. Send her loving energy at this time of transition.

BLESSING AND WISHES

Celebrant: For those of you who wish, please make a single blessing for *Alani* — a word, a phrase.

Song: **'There Is a Season'** (The Byrds)

CANDLE-LIGHTING CEREMONY

Everyone has a candle in a holder in front of them.

Celebrant: Together we light these candles to honour the transition to adulthood, the transition that many of us here have made already, that *Alani* makes today, and as our ancestors have done before us. Today we honour this transition.

All light their candles.

CROSSING THE THRESHOLD

Celebrant: Family and friends,
We are going to make a tunnel of transition — the transition from adolescence to adulthood. Please line up in two rows facing each other, holding your hands over your heads, with fingertips touching those of the people opposite.

Alani will be sent on her journey from one end by her mother. She will pass through the tunnel touching all our lives, and will emerge through the threshold into adult life to be greeted, garlanded and embraced by her older sister, herself an adult.

Alani passes through the tunnel, and crosses the threshold.

Celebrant (all repeat after the celebrant):
   We welcome you into adulthood, *Alani*.
   Our love and blessings go with you.

Celebrant: As the ceremony has now concluded, let the festivities begin!

Everyone shared a meal together, and then danced the night away to the sound of a Latin-American band.

30th Birthday Ceremony

(Inspired by ceremonies created by Lyn Knorr and Mary Hancock)

INTRODUCTION

Celebrant: For thousands of years ceremony has played a key role in all societies around the world, particularly at the times of major or significant transition in people's lives. These ceremonies, or rites of passage, assist people to take that step. From birth our minds and spirits are slowly shaped by a set of values, customs and mythologies specific to our own time and place; they give our lives structure and meaning. The most important spiritual values are usually expressed in ceremony. Tonight we gather to honour *Angeline*, and to celebrate with her as she moves through this rite of passage on her thirtieth birthday. This is the completion of three decades of growth and learning, and she is poised at the beginning point of a new stage in her life, perhaps the most exciting decade of her life.

This ceremony is a moment when we let *Angeline* know that we are gathered here to tell her, that we, her family and friends, are really glad she is part of our lives, that she is a very special and talented person, that we support her and we love her.

LIGHTING THE CANDLE

To honour the past thirty years and the three decades of growth and change, I invite *Angeline*'s godmother, *Marian*, to light the thirtieth birthday candle. As *Marian* lights this candle I invite all of you to reflect on your own growth, your own cycles, and what has been important for you.

READING

Francesca (*Angeline*'s mother) then reads an extract from Jean Bollen's *The Heroine in Every Woman* [see MCR 1].

REFLECTION

Celebrant: Tonight marks a major transition in *Angeline's* life journey. Tonight she honours herself, we honour her, and mark this transition.

I invite you now to think about the connections you have with *Angeline*; to contemplate the relationship you have with her, in a short meditation about and for her.

I invite you also to make a wish for this woman in the prime of her life. Let us all give out loving vibes, and send her loving energy at this moment.

READINGS

Alberto (*Angeline's* brother) reads extracts from *The Desiderata;* and her sister, *Veronica*, reads a quotation from a speech by Nelson Mandela that has always been an inspiration to *Angeline*. (Readings in these ceremonies need to be personally chosen.)

Celebrant: *Angeline*,
Having completed three decades of life, you now move into a new stage, a new challenge and a new complex of choices. Know that your family, your friends, will love you, encourage you and support you, whatever these choices are.

THE WALKWAY OF TRANSITION

(As in the procedure for the 21st birthday ceremony.)

Angeline passes through the walkway, greeting everyone, while one of her favourite songs is played ('One Hand in Her Pocket' by Alanis Morissette). The words of the song are supplied to all present so that they can easily follow it.

Angeline's sisters and her brother:
We welcome you, *Angeline*, to the next exciting decade of your life.
Our love and blessings are with you on your journey.

Final blessing

Celebrant: We will conclude our ceremony for *Angeline* with a Leunig prayer as a blessing for friends and family who have gathered here tonight.

Celebrant: *Steve* has written a special song for *Angeline*, which he and his friend, Tracey, will sing, accompanied by guitars.

RESPONSE AND CELEBRATION

Angeline responds with a short speech.

Everyone then joins in singing 'Happy Birthday', and *Angeline* cuts her birthday cake to three cheers.

Midlife Transition — 49th Birthday Ceremony
(Celebrant, Mary Hancock)

This is the seventh cycle of seven. Those who choose this cycle celebrate the seventh, fourteenth, twenty-first (and so on) birthdays. The forty-ninth is the last in the cycle.

WELCOME AND INTRODUCTION

Celebrant: Welcome to *Lien's* ritual at the equinox to celebrate her forty-ninth birthday, a major transition at midlife.

To make this space special I would like to invoke the energy of the four directions at this time of the equinox — equal day and equal night, a time of harvest, a gathering in, a time of balance.

> *South* — Earth. I invoke the energy of abundance, harvest and nurture.
> *North* — Fire. I invoke the energy of fire and heat, wildness and intensity, the energy that feeds our spirit.
> *West* — Water. I invoke the energy of water: emotions, feelings with the fullness of love.

> *East* — Air. I invoke the energy of the east air, the energy of clarity, insight, razor-sharp thought, poised in its balance at the equinox.

These energies we invoke tonight as we gather and celebrate with *Lien* as she is poised at the threshold of her midlife — moving from one cycle to the next in her life.

HONOURING THE LIFE CYCLES

Celebrant: *Lien,*

I invite you to move into this special circle we have created for you, and to sit by the bow of seven candles. Each candle represents a seven-year period in *Lien*'s life.

This week *Lien* celebrated her forty-ninth birthday, the completion point of seven cycles of growth and learning, and is now poised at the beginning point, the threshold of a new stage in her life — midlife.

To honour the past forty-nine years and the seven cycles of growth and change (seven cycles of seven years each), I invite *Lien* to light her seven rainbow candles — symbols of these seven cycles.

As *Lien* slowly lights these candles, take time to reflect on your own growth, your own cycles. What was important for you from birth to seven, seven to fourteen, fourteen to twenty-one, twenty-one to twenty-eight, twenty-eight to thirty-five, thirty-five to forty-two, forty-two to forty-nine?

HARVEST

Celebrant: *Lien* has now completed these first seven cycles. She is at the threshold again. Before you step over the threshold *Lien*, it is time for you to share with us what you are harvesting in your life, what is in your symbolic basket. Will you share some of your insights and wisdom with us?

Lien brings out a huge basket full of ripe, succulent grapes. She tells her story of her harvest over her seven cycles, and shares her grapes with everyone, as symbols of the harvest.

CROSSING THE THRESHOLD

Celebrant: Having completed your seven-year cycle with the celebration of your forty-ninth birthday, *Lien*, you now move into a new stage in your life.

Please light the new large, single candle as a symbol of the next stage of your life — a crossing of the threshold — and receive this basket of seeds and bulbs, symbolic of what you are seeding, what is gestating, germinating, what is new and beginning, what is hidden away and tucked out of sight, waiting to unfold in the next stage of your life.

Lien, in your newness, in your unfolding, hold these gently and quietly to yourself. May they unfurl like a new fern.

BLESSINGS

Celebrant: *Lien*, as you sit in this new place, in this new unfolding time of your life, on your birthday, we are going to give you the simple gifts of our blessings and wishes.

I invite everyone, when they are ready, to each take a birthday candle, light it, and give *Lien* a wish or blessing at this time of newness and seeding.

To finish this ceremony we will sing the song 'Dear Friends', to honour *Lien* on her forty-ninth birthday, and to honour our friendship with her and each other.

At some forty-ninth birthdays seven relatives and friends are asked to speak about each seven-year period in turn.

My 60th Birthday Ceremony

I hope you will appreciate a personal recollection of a celebration that meant so much to me. It was organised by my daughters, who thought it fitting that their father, a celebrant, should have a ceremony — instead of just talking about them!

★

SONGS AND REMINISCENCES

My three daughters — Genevieve, Natasha, Julia — sang the songs I taught them as little girls ('He's Got the Whole World in His Hands', 'Michael, Row the Boat Ashore', 'Rock My Soul in the Bosom of Abraham').

PROCESSION AND PRESENTATION

My friend Stan Jordan headed a procession through the Fitzroy Gardens holding a big cushion, on which was my Senior's Card; he was accompanied by two drummers (two daughters). Everyone in the gardens stopped and stared!

I was sitting on a chair near the dolphin fountain where, with appropriate bowing and scraping, he presented me with my card, the crux of the ceremony.

READING

My friend Rod Watson read the following reflection:

For All Those Born Before 1945 [MCR 3]

We are survivors.
Consider the changes we have witnessed.
We were before TV, before penicillin, before polio shots,
frozen foods, photocopying, contact lenses, frisbees,
and the pill.
We were before credit cards, split atoms, laser beams and
ballpoint pens, before pantyhose, dishwashers, clothes
dryers, electric blankets, dripdry clothing, and before
man walked on the moon.
We got married first, and then lived together. How
quaint can you be?
We thought fast food was what people ate during Lent,
and outer space was the back of the local theatre.
We were before house husbands, gay rights, computer
dating, dual careers, and computer marriages.
We had never heard of electric typewriters, artificial
hearts, or word processors. Hardware meant
hardware, and software wasn't even a word.

In 1940 'Made in Japan' meant junk, and the term
'making out' referred to how you did in the exam.

Pizza, McDonalds and instant coffee were unheard of in
our day; cigarette smoking was fashionable, grass was
mowed, coke was a cold drink, and pot was
something you cooked in.

Rock music was Grandma's lullaby, and aids were helpers
in the hospitals.

We were certainly not before the difference between the
sexes was discovered, but we were surely before the
sex change.

We made do with what we had.

We were the last generation that was so dumb as to think
you needed a husband to have a baby.

No wonder we are so confused and there is such a
generation gap, and so much more —

but WE SURVIVED.

THE SIX DECADES

Six friends spoke on the six decades of my life: Marj, my wife,
on my earliest years; my friends Giedrius Dryza on my
teenage and high school years, John Murray on my college
years, Rick Barclay on my early celebrant years, Noel Pelly on
my years with *Dance Australia* magazine, and Stan Jordan (my
running and jogging partner, and accountant) on recent times.
Each of the six spoke about a ten-year period.

SPECIAL SONG

My youngest daughter, Julia, a graduate of the Melbourne
Conservatorium of Music in singing, then sang 'Oh My
Beloved Father' (Puccini). (By this time I was mass of jelly
blubber.)

PRESENTATION

For over twenty years I have had hanging on my wall an
enlarged school photo of the five girls (my three daughters
and my two stepdaughters, Melissa and Rachel) at a very

happy time in their lives. They have always teased me about it, and I had the impression they didn't like seeing it there. But to me it symbolised the happy home and lifestyle I had provided for them, so on the wall it stayed. The final part of the ceremony was when the girls presented me with another enlarged and framed photo taken twenty years later with the five of them in the same formation. (That sent me out of control, too!)

'BIRTHDAY BOY' SPEECH

I then made a speech.

One hundred family and friends came to the picnic in the Fitzroy Gardens. It was an event I will always remember!

8 Transitions and Life Cycles

Career Transitions

Mary Hancock here describes a ceremony she wrote for a career change. This framework could also be adapted for:
- the opening of a new business
- a person forced to leave a career because of redundancy, or when accepting a package.

> Diane had had twenty-two years' experience as a nurse in a range of hospitals. At the age of forty, she decided to make a career change, and set up her own business as an independent nurse practitioner in private practice. She felt that this was a very important event in her life, particularly in her career, and wanted to mark this with a formal ceremony, and thus acknowledge it as a major transition.
>
> Diane invited thirty-five of her colleagues, family and friends to her new premises for her ceremony. On their invitations, each person was asked to bring a simple affirmation or wish for her new business venture.
>
> The celebrant welcomed everyone, and in the introduction briefly talked about the importance of making and honouring new directions in work. For the rest of this

ceremony the celebrant's role was one of facilitator or co-ordinator.

Diane shared her vision of her new career, acknow-ledging her hopes and fears. Then her guests gave their affirmations, thoughts and wishes, each in turn lighting one of the small candles framing her business plan in the centre of the room. Diane then cut a large ribbon, sym-bolising her crossing the threshold into a new business venture. Champagne toasts were made.

The ceremony was completed with Diane giving a rose to all her guests in thanks for their support in affirm-ing her new business move.

After the ceremony Diane felt quite transformed. It marked the point of change in her career, it affirmed her career choices and it was empowering to see her business plan symbolically honoured and energised.

★

Ceremonies for redundancy or taking a package could incor-porate prepared testimonials by management, colleagues and staff, and a significant engraved gift.

The person should prepare a response.

Another suggestion is for all present to sing together in a spirit of camaraderie.

A special feast or dinner should follow.

Graduation of Celebrants

(This ceremony, devised by the students, was held after a five-week course on celebrancy conducted by the author.)

PROCESSION

The invited celebrant lights the candle held by the course instructor, and the graduates process in, to music such as 'The Grand March' from Verdi's *Aida*.

The celebrant gives each person a candle, and the gradu-ates move on to light their candle from the instructor's, and then take their seats.

READINGS

Various graduates read quotations, such as the following:

From The Prophet [TR 1]

No man can reveal to you aught but that which already lies half asleep in the dawning of your knowledge.

The teacher who walks in the shadow of the temple, among his followers, gives not of his wisdom but rather of his faith and his lovingness.

If he is indeed wise he does not bid you enter the house of his wisdom, but rather leads you to the threshold of your own mind.

The astronomer may speak to you of his understanding of space, but he cannot give you his understanding.

The musician may sing to you of the rhythm which is in all space, but he cannot give you the ear which arrests the rhythm, nor the voice that echoes it.

Kahlil Gibran

From On Education [TR 2]

I will point you out the right path
of a virtuous and Noble Education:
laborious indeed at the first ascent,
but else so smooth, so green,
so full of goodly prospect,
and melodious sounds on every side,
that the harp of Orpheus was not more charming.

John Milton

Proverbs 1:20–2 [TR 3]

Wisdom calls aloud in the streets,
She raises her voice in the public squares,
She calls out at the street corners,
She delivers her message at the city gates.
'You ignorant people,
How much longer will mockers revel in their mocking
and fools hold knowledge contemptible?'

Ecclesiastes 6:18 ff [TR 4]

My son, from your earliest youth choose instruction,
and till your hair is white you will keep finding wisdom.
Cultivate her like the ploughman and the sower,
and wait for her fine harvest
for in tilling her you will toil a little while,
but very soon you will be eating her crops.

PRESENTATION OF CERTIFICATES

The names of the graduates are announced, one by one, by a tutor, and the course instructor presents each person with a certificate.

The candles are left behind, still alight.

THE AFFIRMATION

The celebrant asks all the graduates to stand and make the following affirmation together.

I affirm that I will build positively
on the learning experience of these five weeks.

I commit myself to preparing well for ceremonies,
officiating with attention and awareness,
staying sensitive to the needs of culture
and the happiness of people.

I will attempt to broaden the vision of the community
on the need for celebrating the broad range of events
that make up human life.

I commit myself to reinforcing the professional
    friendships
I have made in this place.

The candles are extinguished, and the course instructor gives a short speech of congratulation.

The celebrant then invites everyone to a ceremonial drink, and proposes a toast.

House Dedication

Des and Jennifer Lambert purchased a unit in East Melbourne. It had a very special appeal for them, and they wanted to celebrate taking it over in a special ceremony. Elements of this ceremony can be used to 'make a special place'.

A personal introduction to such ceremonies should be, and only can be, written after a moderate amount of research and collaboration!

INTRODUCTION

All the guests gather in the foyer, outside the front door.

Celebrant: Friends of Jennifer and Des,
East Melbourne is a very special part of the universe, and the particular block of units known as Belgravia is a very special part of that.

Can you imagine this block of units in the 1940s when they were first built? They would have been the quintessence of postwar luxury, a residence for the finest.

They were lovingly restored and refurbished in 1992 by the much-publicised businessman Geoff Lord, with all the exquisite touches that only a totally committed top executive could give.

What lovelier aspect could we have than a unit in East Melbourne that overlooks a beautiful park, and has easy access to Australia's greatest sporting venue (the Melbournt Cricket Ground) and all this city's parks and facilities? In short, East Melbourne is a special alcove, almost in the centre of, but removed from, the worst features of the world's 'most livable city'.

There are some good personal vibes as well. Jennifer and Des have a home in Queensland, and they have travelled all over the world, but East Melbourne and its surrounds say something very special to them. Even the name Belgravia says something to Des. During his years in London he lived in the suburb of Belgravia, and had a wonderful time there.

It is beautifully spooked in another way. Five is their lucky number and this is Unit 25, number 155. Des was actually born on the 15/5/1950 at 5 a.m., so for that reason the place resonates with fives. Five is one of Jen's lucky numbers, too, as she was born on 25 August. When she was born, she had five fingers on each hand and a similar number of toes on each foot!

She loves the view from every window — this is not common in near-city apartments. Dappled sunlight comes through the trees in the morning, and she feels that she is living in a treehouse — the possums frequently drop by to say hello!

We are part of their lives, too. They like the people of East Melbourne — around here we all live interesting lives, and we are a constant source of inspiration!

Let us enter this place, and make it special.

All are then given a glass of sherry.

Celebrant: This drink of sherry is a traditional Anglo-Saxon drink of welcome. Please drink to a welcome to all from our hosts, and drink to this foyer, the threshold of hospitality.

All drink a toast.

Celebrant: We will first of all revive some ancient cultural traditions. Anglo-Saxons purify with salt, and bring joy with rosewater. The Chinese, in the *feng shui* tradition, do it with oranges and lemons, so we will use all these customs in dedicating all the rooms of this house.
I ask one of the guests, Frank, to dedicate the foyer.

Frank (armed with salt, and water laced with roses, lemons and oranges, with a leafy sprig for sprinkling the water):
I hereby sprinkle this salt and, in doing so,
I rid this room of all evil vibes, feelings and associations,
and declare it cleansed and clean.

I also sprinkle this rosewater,
further flavoured with lemons and orange,
as a symbol that we will make this a room of happiness,
joy, good luck and good feeling.

I call on everyone present to focus their spiritual feelings, and bless this place.

May there be love and light and harmony within this room.

Des then carries Jen across the threshold into the living area.

Everyone proceeds to the dining/livingroom, and the balcony; then the kitchen, the bathroom and the bedrooms. The ritual is repeated for each room by a different person.

After all the rooms have been dedicated, everyone meets in the loungeroom.

CUTTING OF THE CAKE

Candles are lit as a symbol of the household gods and spirits coming to everyone. Then, heated symbolically by the hearth candle, the welcome cake is cut and shared by everyone.

Jen and Des make welcoming speeches to their guests, and all make celebratory toasts. This is followed by everyone singing together (words are provided) Guy Mitchell's song, 'There Is Always Room at Our House'.

Recommitment
(Celebrant: Mary Hancock)

GREETINGS AND WELCOME

Celebrant: We are here today to celebrate and honour *Lois* and *Tony*'s love, and to acknowledge the long journey of this relationship.

Tony and *Lois* were married in England on 22 June 1969. Soon after, they came to New Zealand to begin a new life there.

Today, after a long period of separation, they are together again and want to honour and celebrate their relationship, to acknowledge its changes and to reclaim it in a new way. Their separation agreement, made several years ago, is a symbol of their changes. It is a reflection of each being their own person.

TAROT CARD

Celebrant: *Lois* and *Tony* have chosen a card from the ancient tarot as a symbol for them of their love and their relationship — you will have seen the card on their invitation. It is the twentieth card, the judgement card. It represents our ability to give birth to new forms in both family and career situations. It reminds us to look at the history we have shared, and to forgive ourselves and others for the judgements we are making about what we are doing or not doing in our lives.

This is a very appropriate symbol for *Tony* and *Lois* today as they have both been giving birth to new forms in their careers, and in the new directions of their relationship.

TAPESTRY OF CONNECTIONS

Celebrant: This is not an exclusive ceremony for *Lois* and *Tony*. They both want to acknowledge the key role of *Hannah*, their daughter, and you, their friends, in their lives.

In doing this, we acknowledge and honour all our connections with *Lois* and *Tony*, and weave together our rich tapestry of many interlocking threads.

Tony and *Lois* will begin; please follow with your woven interconnections too.

GIFTS

Celebrant: *Tony* and *Lois* wish to affirm all the wonderful bonds and connections between you, their family and friends, and they have a gift for each of you.

Lois and *Tony,* together, distribute gifts all brightly wrapped from a large hamper.

EXCHANGE OF RINGS (Hannah is the ring-bearer)
Celebrant: In honouring their love, and in celebrating the renewal of their relationship, *Lois* and *Tony* wish to exchange rings with each other.

We will pass the rings around, and ask, as you each hold them and warm them, that you silently give your own blessings and loving energy to the rings.

Music is played as the rings are blessed. The rings are exchanged in silence.

WISHING CUP

Celebrant: We will pass around a wishing cup, a loving cup. Please drink from it, honouring all the loving bonds between us here today, and make a wish aloud for *Tony* and *Lois* if you would like to.

TREE PLANTING

Celebrant: We will now adjourn to the garden for *Lois* and *Tony* to plant a tree, as a symbol of their love, and an honouring of the new commitment in their relationship.

FIRE LIGHTING

Celebrant: Another symbol for *Tony* and *Lois* of their new commitment together is the home that they have built here together.

Today they wish to ritually light the fire in the hearth, for the first time as a symbol of their joint spirits.

As they light this fire, let us light the candles all around us, affirming this beautiful space that *Lois*, *Tony* and *Hannah* share together.

From The Tao of Pooh   [R]

The clouds above us join and separate,
The breeze in the courtyard leaves and returns.
Life is like that, so why not relax?
Who can stop us from celebrating?

Step Acceptance Ceremony

This can be a ceremony in its own right, or incorporated into a wedding ceremony.

I want to start by telling you Martin's story. I know his mother (she is a celebrant). For three years Martin resented his father's new wife. He blamed her for replacing his mother, monopolising his father, and for 'taking away' his father's love. Over four years his stepmother put in an effort: she played golf with Martin, she interested herself in his music — and stepmother and stepson became friends. They talked.

Two years later she died, and Martin grieved deeply.

Martin suggested to me that he should have been told at the beginning what his stepmother clearly explained to him later on — that she was only there at his father's invitation; that resentment should not be directed at her; that as he was young and she was one of two adults in the home, she had to enjoy a certain level of authority, and she was entitled to tell him not to leave his towel on the bathroom floor, otherwise the house could never run properly. She never wanted, or would want, to replace his mother in his life, but as she had married his father she had an obligation, as did Martin, to have a relationship of respect, possibly a relationship of friendship, even a relationship of love in the special sense that it did not threaten the relationship he remembered with his mother.

INTRODUCTION

This introduction should contain the following messages:

- Everyone deserves respect, until they clearly demonstrate they do not deserve it.
- Everyone can do with friendship — life is too short anyway, so why not try it?
- Change in families is emotional and difficult; tolerance, understanding and patience are needed from both parties.
- Stepparents are only there because of the breakup of the parents, and at the invitation of a parent.

- The place of natural parents in the hearts and minds of children should never be threatened or put down.
- Stepparents should have a certain authority in a house, but they shouldn't push it too far, and the stepchildren should respect their place and the level of authority that is necessary.

A commitment pledge should be given by the stepparent to the stepchild, and vice versa, followed by an exchange of gifts, and a drink from a 'cup of friendship'.

Both should then shake hands or embrace, to everyone's applause.

COMMITMENT (as part of a wedding ceremony when a parent remarries)

Celebrant: Ladies and Gentlemen.

Today *Marta* marries *Gary*. But we all know that it this isn't the only relationship established today. There is a whole new network of relationships set up by this marriage, as there is in any marriage. Perhaps the most important family relationship that is now established is that between *Gary* and *Brad*, *Marta*'s son. Steprelationships are often difficult for all sorts of reasons, but with the right attitude they can be very helpful and productive.

So I ask you, *Gary*, will you do your best to assist *Brad* in whatever way you can during these important years of growth? Will you respect his relationship with his parents, yet be aware of your important place in his life and treat him with interest, care, concern, fairness and respect?

Gary: I will.

Celebrant: *Brad*, now that your family will include *Gary* as a parent to you, will you treat him with respect and fairness, and do your best to have the best and friendliest relationship possible?

Brad: I will.

Gary and *Brad* exchange gifts to seal the commitment, shaking hands or embracing.

(If part of a wedding, the ceremony continues.)

Divorce Ceremony

This was an unusual divorce ceremony in that both parties wanted it, and agreed to it. The striking aspect was that thoughts were expressed, values affirmed, and mutual appreciation displayed in a way that could not effectively occur in private conversations.

Celebrant: We are playing this song 'It's Over, Goodbye' for its general sentiments, and not every word applies literally to *Ina* and *Ron*.

The words of the song were provided so that everyone could easily follow it.

INTRODUCTION

Celebrant: Welcome to you all.
We come together this evening, not in joy but in acceptance. The purpose of tonight's ceremony is to heal hearts, to forgive the past, to celebrate the past, but, most importantly, to release the future.

Ina and *Ron* have decided to separate and divorce, and so we are meeting here to mark this important transition. The great breaks in life's pattern, major changes in life, take a great emotional toll. From such change we do well to retain as much love, forgiveness and courage as possible. From such change we do well to strengthen ourselves inwardly, reinforce our positive attitudes, and realise the truth that 'When one door shuts, another one opens'. Sometimes better ones open.

Celebrant to the couple: *Ron* and *Ina*,
It is clear that your marriage is over and finished. Even though this is the case, you should see it not as an ending but a new beginning.

Celebrant to the son and daughter: *Peter* and *Julia*,
This could not have been a pleasant experience for you, and everyone knows it. You know that your parents love you, and they are deeply sorry for any pain you may have been caused.

No one person has the wisdom to judge the causes of a marriage breakup. Your parents especially thank you, and ask you to continue to show understanding, tolerance, support and love to both of them. You should take seriously the reassurance that you are not the cause of, or any part of, your parents' intensely personal decision.

You will always be part of both new lives that *Ina* and *Ron*, as individuals, will continue develop.

Celebrant to Don's mother: *Dorothy,*
Both *Ina* and *Ron* want to thank you fully and sincerely for everything you have done for both of them, and for *Julia* and *Peter*, throughout the marriage. You have always been there with your love and support, and tonight they wish to place this on record, and express the hope that it will continue, at an appropriate level.

Celebrant to the couple: *Ina* and *Ron,*
This ceremony is a reminder that you must accept the separation, the finalisation of the marriage, fully and completely. Do this carefully and peaceably, and in a civilised manner.

You should care for yourselves so that any hurts will heal, just as one cares for oneself at the time of any physical illness.

Your union was an important part of your lives — it produced the two children of whom you are so proud. When you look back, do so with respect and honour.

When you have established your new futures, and when your emotions are settled, hopefully you will be able to communicate easily as friends and parents.

Your marriage was a time of achievement, it had many times of happiness and joy and love. Remember this time positively.

STATEMENT OF DIVORCE

Ina to Ron:
> I release you from our marriage.
> Please forgive me any hurts I have caused you,
> as I forgive you.
> I wish you well for your future.

Ron to Ina:
> I release you from our marriage.
> Please forgive me any hurts I have caused you,
> as I forgive you.
> I wish you well for your future.

Celebrant: I now call on you, *Ina* and *Ron*, to burn your marriage certificate in this bowl, symbolising the end of your marriage.

The marriage certificate is burnt.

Celebrant: *Ina* and *Ron*, please now light your individual candles from the original marriage candle. By this you will symbolise the taking of the good memories and achievements from your marriage as enlightenment and strength, as you now pursue your individual courses.

Ina lights her candle from the main candle, as does Ron. Together they then blow out the main candle.
> A few moments of silence are observed while music is played.

Celebrant: *Ina* and *Ron*,
> I now declare you divorced,
> and wish you well for your future.

Changing a Name

Ted Logan, a prominent Melbourne celebrant, wrote this ceremony for a lady who did not like her given name, and wanted to change it. She invited all her family and friends — a big crowd!

INTRODUCTION

Celebrant: Ladies and Gentlemen,
Thank you for your attendance on this special occasion, and the respect, love and support you have shown to our friend — for the moment I will continue to call her *'Mary' Sullivan*.

We are here to take part in a ceremony in which the name *Mary* will be renounced, and expunged from daily use and record documents, and a new name will take its place, to be used by everyone in the future in all situations.

The name change has already been lodged and registered legally by Deed Poll; this public ceremony will reinforce the change, and re-emphasise the importance of this event in the lives of *Mrs Sullivan* and her family.

Shakespeare had some interesting comments to make on the subject of names. In *Romeo and Juliet* he states: 'What's in a name? That which we call a rose by any other name would smell as sweet'. While this is no doubt true, it is also true that some names are more melodic, or carry stronger connotations or evoke deeper emotions than others. Through usage, names pick up hurtful or unhappy memories; it would be unthinkable today for any parents to call their child Satan or Hitler.

On the other hand, in one of his plays Shakespeare also says:

From Othello [TR 5]

Good name in man or woman, dear my lord,
Is the immediate jewel of their souls;
Who steals my purse,
steals trash; 'tis something, nothing.
'Twas mine, 'tis his, and has been slaves to thousands;
But he that filches from me my good name
Robs me of that which not enriches him
And makes me poor indeed.

The name Mary has some bitter memories for *Mrs Sullivan* (the word Mary itself in the Hebrew language means 'bitter') and indeed this has been the experience that *Mrs Sullivan* has had to carry, sad, traumatic and tearful times, with this name.

Since her remarriage circumstances have changed for the better. She has become much more outgoing and extroverted; a more sympathetic, caring and loving person; happy in herself and in her husband, and happy with her children *Michael* and *Eleanor*; and with her friends *Jayne* and *Karen*, and her other friends.

In recent times *Mrs Sullivan* has been greatly assisted by her mentor and friend *Stephanie*, whose wise counselling sessions have been of tremendous help to her in planning her future paths and goals.

The change of name is a symbol of the changes in her life; but more than a symbol of the past, it is the promise of a different and better life carried forward into the future.

Up to this point I have refrained from using the new name that *Mrs Sullivan* has chosen for herself. It is *Sara*, and from now on this is the name we will all use.

The first recorded Sara was the wife of the patriarch Abraham mentioned in the Bible. It is stated in the book of Genesis that she was a good-looking woman. Abraham at one stage said, 'Behold now, I know that thou art a fair woman to look upon'. Sarah bore a son, Isaac, when she was ninety years old! We won't wish this problem onto our *Sara*!

The name Sara, I'm told, means 'princess'.

Famous Saras have included Sarah Churchill (the wife of the first Duke of Marlborough, and a family name for the Churchills); Sara Dane was the main character in a book of that name about an enterprising woman pioneer in the early days of Sydney; Sarah Vaughan is well known as a singer; Sara Maitland is a novelist; and who can ignore Sara Lee, purveyor of puddings, pies and pastries! We now have another Sara to join this distinguished group of people.

NAMING CEREMONY

Celebrant: Would everyone please now join me as we symbolically call *Sara* by her new, reborn name for the first time? Please repeat the words I use after me.

All repeat:

We all agree to call you *Sara Sullivan*.
So we therefore name you *Sara*.
We wish you long life and happiness
in a loving and peaceful world.
May you bring joy to your family and friends,
and have a happy and successful life.
May you contribute to making this world
a better and happier place.

CEREMONY OF REJUVENATION

Celebrant: The phoenix was a mythical bird of the ancient Egyptians, which, at the end of its 500-year life cycle, consumed itself in the flames of its funeral pyre, then rose up from the fire as a young bird miraculously reborn. All of the pains, sorrows and unhappy memories of its past life were thus purged away, and a new life, free from these past encumbrances, could then begin.

Sara has inscribed on this paper all the traumas and wrongs that to her were associated with her past life and past name. She is now coming forward to symbolically burn the document in the urn, and, with the flames, may all the unhappy memories of her life disappear like the smoke from the fire.

Then, like the phoenix, *Sara* will be reborn from the ashes of her previous life into a bright and happy future.

Sara burns the document.

Celebrant: Ladies and Gentlemen,
Please raise your glasses, and join me in a toast:
>To *Sara Sullivan*,
>To a long and happy life,
>and to a successful future!

To close the formal part of today's proceedings, I now invite *Sara* to say a few words.

9 Sorry Ceremony*

Celebrants are now realising that they should show leadership, and use their experience in public ceremonies of joy, sorrow and reconciliation. Here is one example of such a ceremony, the 'Sorry' ceremony — part of the reconciliation of Aboriginal and white Australians.

Introduction and Welcome

RESPONSES

Celebrant:
> Why are you here today?
> Why have you come to this place?

Aboriginal people:
> We are here because this is our place.
> Our people have lived here for countless generations.
> This land and its waters have given life and culture, and
> identity.

All the women:
> We are child-bearing people.
> We give life and love.
> We are here because of the pain of mothers whose
> children were stolen from them.

All the young people:
> We are children who are glad we have parents who
> love us.

---

*Reproduced with thanks to the Reverend Martin Reilly and colleagues, and the City of Banyule.

We are here because so many children were taken from their loving parents.

All the men:

We honour mateship and a fair go.

We are here because of our desire to be reconciled with Aborigine and Torres Strait Islander brothers and sisters, and to see justice given.

Everyone:

We are here at the bidding of our organisations within the city of Banyule

to commemorate the culture of Australia's indigenous people,

to remember the wrongs,

to seek reconciliation,

and to envision a future of peace and justice for all Australians.

Commemoration

All take part in presenting Aboriginal music and dance, in remembering and sharing stories, and in viewing the video *Bringing Them Home.*

A period of silence follows.

Apology

While all stand, an apology is given by the mayor of the city, on behalf of its citizens, and a signed Sorry Book is presented to the Aboriginal people.

The Aboriginal people respond with their vision of the future.

Commitment (all standing)

We stand together as one body,

to acknowledge our history

and the pain it has caused for many people.

We are united in our commitment to healing those hurts
and learning from them.
As we continue this journey of healing and hope,
we will be there for each other.
Together we look forward to building a better future
based on hope, trust and friendship.

Celebration

An appropriate song celebrating freedom and friendship is
then sung by everyone.

Celebrant: We have here a picture of three birds: the eagle,
the swallow and the dove. They are symbolic of the groups
involved today, and lead us in the way of peace and reconciliation.

Bunjil, the eagle, is the social totem of the Wurundjeri
people. It represents a spiritual being with spiritual power.
Bunjil taught all the laws of life and behaviour to the first man
and woman, which ensured that the culture would continue
for eternity.

The City of Banyule has as its logo the 'Welcome Swallow'.
It suggests festivity and liveliness, while acknowledging the
artistic heritage of Banyule. The arc on the logo is a stylised
hill, affirming connection with the land.

These two symbols, side by side, affirm our mutual commitment as we stand in the present and prepare for the future.

The dove of peace, holding an olive branch, draws the two
together to begin a new era of co-operation and respect.

We recognise that today is not the end, but a beginning.
An apology is not enough without a commitment to reform
our ways to respect and include each other in our lives.

You are all invited to place on the picture one of the dots
you have received, maybe even sign your name, stylising a traditional art form, yet bringing a communal commitment to
this process of reconciliation and peace. Placing the dot is a
symbolic act of commitment to a peaceful future for all
Australians.

Part 3

FUNERALS

10 The Personal Funeral

The now established life-centred or personal funeral sprang from the conviction that the funeral should primarily recognise and pay tribute to the life of the deceased person.

I personally dislike the expression 'the funeral service is for the living'. In one sense, I hardly think about the living when I am preparing a funeral. I think about the life of the person to whom I must pay tribute. I further think that the conventional funeral is a most inadequate response — 15 to 25 minutes to put on record a whole life of loving work and achievement!

So it is incumbent on a celebrant, of whatever kind, to put time into the preparation. The well-prepared funeral offers the best kind of comfort, support and sense of hope to the survivors.

Many funeral ceremonies fail to focus carefully on the lifetime achievements of the person who has died. When this happens, the true needs of the bereaved are not recognised, the ritual becomes meaningless and adds to grief.

A personal funeral service, properly prepared, checked with the family, and delivered with care and sensitivity, helps people live through their feelings, recognise the reality of death, and assists grieving people to work toward living normally without that person.

HOW DID IT ALL START?

It was in 1976. I had been a civil marriage celebrant for nearly two years, and was loving every minute of it. Weddings — what could be more socially stimulating than to join a group of people for a happy celebration when everyone is at their friendliest and best? A celebrant enjoys a special pleasure — you help to create a memorable occasion.

Yet, every now and then, someone would pull me aside from the jollity and ask me whether, if called upon, I would officiate at a non-religious funeral. I can remember being surprised at these questions — twenty-five years ago you did not mention death or dying unless you had to.

I dodged and twisted, wriggled and joked. I was reluctant. I knew though, that the same reasoning, the same philosophy that underlies the civil marriage underlies the civil funeral. There is a deep human need to surround important occasions in life with ritual, symbolism, expressions of belief and feeling, and festivities or gatherings. Non-religious and non-churchgoing people have the same need for a meaningful cultural celebration as churchgoing people do for a religio-cultural celebration. If there is a human need for one, there is a human need for the other. If a couple do not want the church or a clergyman in life, how in all genuineness can they ask for them in death?

Then one day, quite suddenly, it happened. The phone rang: it was the bridegroom from a marriage at which I had officiated two months previously. 'It's Roy here, Dally. Helen has just died. In view of her beliefs, we've all talked it over and we've decided to ask you to officiate at her funeral. If you don't do it, I don't know what we'll do. Will you?' Helen was only twenty-two, and I had got to know her quite well. They were my kind of people. I can remember procrastinating, but from the first I knew I had to do it.

THE FIRST FUNERAL

This was my first funeral, and, from what I can ascertain, the first celebrant funeral in Australia. I will call it non-religious, but to be more accurate it was a non-Christian funeral. Helen was religious, but her religion was a mixture of many, including some Eastern religions.

The best way to describe what I did was to say I wrote a panegyric, a eulogy or a biography, or whatever you like to call it. I spoke to her husband, mother, father, family and friends. I found out what her favourite quotations were, took some thoughts from her marriage service, and quoted from some posters on her bedroom wall. I put it all together in the best way I could.

It was a bit of a shock when I arrived at the funeral parlour chapel. It was filled to overflowing (the funerals of young people usually are), and the directors had set up loudspeakers for the people who had to stand outside.

I spoke about Helen, her life, her loves, her achievement, her beliefs. At suitable times I quoted her favourite verses of poetry and pieces of literature. I took this idea mainly from President Kennedy's funeral — a format that had impressed me some years earlier.

The ceremony lasted about 25–30 minutes at the funeral parlour, followed by 5–10 minutes at the crematorium.

It was, like all funerals, emotionally draining, yet I found it very rewarding. What amazed me, really amazed me, on this occasion and since, is the number of people who came up to me and told me what it did for them to have me talk about Helen accurately and authentically. Quite a number urged me to keep doing funeral ceremonies.

I was invited back to the house for refreshments, and found myself surrounded by a group of people. Helen's brother-in-law, Dennis, was particularly intense with me.

'You just have to keep doing this', he said to me passionately. 'You really must. This is much more important than doing marriages.'

Since that conversation I must have had thousands of conversations about funeral ceremonies. The overwhelming impression I get is that most people are very dissatisfied with what they hear at funerals. Sometimes there is an animosity at inappropriate words said, at names wrongly stated, or facts inaccurately reported, that borders on the violent.

A SAD EXPERIENCE

In the late 1970s a Sydney man told me about the funeral of a prominent exiled black African who had suffered and been exiled in the cause of civil rights for his countrymen. A clergyman was asked to officiate at the funeral who did not know the man. He arrived about ten minutes before the ceremony, and began his preparation. He gathered a few brief facts about the deceased. In the context of a church ritual that was not consonant with the beliefs of the dead person he attempted to personalise the ceremony by these brief remarks, which he got mixed up. He pronounced the deceased's name incorrectly, and, among other errors, mistakenly referred to the man as an American Negro.

The large gathering was distressed and hostile at the whole affair. There was a spontaneous reaction: the mourners stopped the coffin on the church steps and demanded that proper words of tribute be said. After some acrimony an understanding was reached, and five or six of the dead man's friends spoke spontaneously in turn (on the steps) of the man's achievements, ideals, values and personal qualities. The funeral was then allowed to proceed.

FEELINGS OF ANTIPATHY

On another occasion I was asked to officiate at a funeral being arranged by the grand-daughter of an old lady. I sat down at the kitchen table, and immediately sensed an atmosphere of deep emotional antipathy.

'What are you going to say about my grandmother?' she asked aggressively.

'I don't know', said I, truthfully. 'Whatever you tell me, I guess.'

Then it came all out. This was the fourth funeral in a year in which she had been involved. She hated funeral directors, clergymen, crematorium officials — everyone. So I listened to her story, and each of her three complaint stories started in a similar way: 'My mother was such and such, and you know what that buffoon said?'My grandfather for his whole life did this, yet in the middle of the service this clown said ...'

Except in those limited and select areas where professional Federation celebrants operate, talk to anyone about funeral ceremonies and you will hear stories of no words said when they should have been, the wrong words said, inappropriate references, embarrassing exaggerations and distressing inaccuracies. The point that came home clearly to me was that relatives and friends want the deceased to be paid proper tribute. Inappropriate words add distress to grief and leave lasting resentment.

I would like to make a point clear here. The clergy, who, until twenty years ago, almost exclusively officiated at funerals, have been criticised by the people with whom I had discussions. I believe, however, that they are not basically at fault. They were pressured into doing ceremonies for non-believers who did not appreciate them, and for non-churchgoers who did not support them. Yet they were offered absurdly low fees to do funerals on the outdated and erroneous premise that the person supported them as a member of a congregation during their lifetime. Years ago this used to happen — almost everyone went to church. Not so now.

One Melbourne clergyman I know solved the problem very simply. He prepares all funerals well. For registered members of his congregation he accepts no stipend; for non-members he charges a professional fee.

In the 1970s when I consulted Lionel Murphy, the founder of the Australian Civil Celebrant programme, and then a Judge of the High Court, he insisted that some celebrants must officiate at funerals and, lest standards of preparation drop, the fee must be at least double that conventionally charged for weddings.

These days prominent non-churchgoers have wonderful funerals with an array of excellent speakers paying prepared and moving tributes. But few people recognise that, before celebrants, eulogies were almost unheard of at funeral ceremonies, and secular funerals were extremely rare, and unknown and unavailable to most people.

EASING THE PAIN AND GRIEF

Initially most authorised marriage celebrants were violently opposed to the idea of conducting funerals. A group of us decided to go this way, and soon found that our experience in this work was much more satisfying than anything we had ever done before. Why was this so? Obviously we were filling a need. I think, however, that it has to be expressed more deeply than this. Someone loved has died. The pain of loss and grief is great. It is very important to pay tribute, to put on record, to keep tangibly, at least in a small way, the life that has been lived.

An appropriate funeral ceremony, a properly prepared eulogy, alleviates the pain. It eases the grief. One lady wrote to me, 'You turned a distressing event into a beautiful memory'.

PREPARATION

To officiate at a good funeral is to do nothing extraordinary. This is how we go about it.

The celebrant must visit the family. The family and friends gather, and the celebrant interviews them. It is always good to get three or four, or more, opinions of the person who has died; different members of the family have varying insights, memories and opinions.

From these facts we write a eulogy or biography. Once prepared, the eulogy is read back to the family, and corrected so that it is one hundred per cent accurate.

A question that I often have to face is on the personal element in a funeral: 'You did not know the person, how can you talk about him/her?'

Those of us who consider ourselves professionals take pains to prepare as well as we can.

After you meet a group of people and they tell you about a person, at a certain stage you cross a barrier, you feel you 'know' the person. At this stage it does become personal. In a sense the celebrant is a biographer.

Celebrants now quite often work with clergymen and women, the latter providing the religious ritual where appropriate, and the celebrant recording the life and achievements of the person at an arranged time during the religious ceremony.

ASSISTING THE GRIEVING PROCESS

One night I was asked to visit a family where the just-retired father had died. I met the wife, the daughter and son-in-law and, after the usual courtesies, we sat down to a couple of hours' discussion about Dad. They were most helpful and co-operative, spoke freely, and were extremely easy people to oblige. I had just arrived home about 10.30 pm when the phone rang. The daughter was on the phone, overcome with relief. She wanted to thank me for getting them talking. Apparently for the two days since the death no one had spoken a word to the other. They did not know what to say. All their thoughts and feelings were bottled up, so the discussion with me was a great relief for them. Her mother, she told me, was now sleeping peacefully for the first time for three nights.

This experience brought home to me that we were assisting people in the grieving process by inviting the bereaved to talk. This is not the prime purpose of the interview, and I think that if I was just a well-meaning friend who had said 'Let's talk', I would probably have got nowhere.

CULTURAL NEEDS

My feeling about celebrants is rather idealistic. Even though everything I am saying applies the world over, it is within Australia that this initiative of celebrants conducting funeral ceremonies began. We see it as a cultural challenge.

The human need is for moving music, the beauty of well-written words, and symbolism — this is what I mean by cultural; it is not necessarily religious. The civil celebrant has the task of developing and presenting that which brings out the best emotional and social responses. Selecting the best of literature, music, and symbolism for a ceremony, in consultation with the family, is the important part of the civil celebrant's work.

Quotations from literature vary greatly, and selecting and suggesting the most appropriate poetry and prose is important. People, of course, may appreciate the very simple or the very sublime and/or the very classical.

A funeral of an Australian drover included the following lines by Banjo Paterson:

From Clancy of the Overflow [FR 1]

For the drover's life has pleasures that the townsfolk
 never know,
And the bush has friends to meet him, and their kindly
 voices greet him
In the murmur of the breezes and the river on its bars.
And he sees the vision splendid, of the sunlit plains
 extended,
And at night the wondrous glory of the everlasting stars.

A lover of Walt Whitman wanted the following lines — an express wish before she died:

From When Lilacs Last in the Dooryard Bloom'd [FR 2]

When lilacs last in the dooryard bloom'd,
And the great star early droop'd in the western sky in
 the night.
I mourn'd, and yet shall mourn with ever-returning
 spring.

Come lovely and soothing death,
Undulate round the world, serenely arriving, arriving
In the day, in the night, to all, to each,
Sooner or later, delicate death.

Prais'd be the fathomless universe,
For life and joy, and for objects and knowledge curious,
And for love, sweet love — but praise! praise! praise!
For the sure-enwinding arms of cool-enfolding death.

The family of one man felt that J. H. Newman's famous description of a gentleman fitted him perfectly:

From Idea of a University [FR 3]

The true gentleman in like manner carefully avoids
whatever may cause a jar or a jolt in the minds of those
with whom he is cast — all clashing of opinion, or
collision of feeling, all restraint, or suspicion, or gloom,
or resentment; his great concern being to make every
one at their ease and at home. He has his eyes on all his
company; he is tender towards the bashful; gentle towards
the distant, and merciful towards the absurd; he can
recollect to whom he is speaking; he guards against
unseasonable allusions, or topics which may irritate;
he is seldom prominent in conversation, and never
wearisome. He makes light of favours while he does
them, and seems to be receiving when he is conferring.

There are also many lovers of the words of Kahlil Gibran:

From The Prophet [FR 4]

'You would know the secret of death, but how shall you
    find it unless you seek it in the heart of life?
The owl whose night-bound eyes are blind unto the day
    cannot unveil the mystery of light.
If you would indeed behold the spirit of death, open
    your hearts wide unto the body of life.
For life and death are one, even as the river and the sea
    are one.
In the depths of your hopes and desires lies your silent
    knowledge of the beyond; and like seeds dreaming
    beneath the snow your heart dreams of spring.
Trust the dreams, for in them is hidden the gate to eternity.
Your fear of death is but the trembling of the shepherd
    when he stands before the king whose hand is to be
    laid upon him in honour ...
For what is it to die but to stand naked in the wind and
    to melt into the sun?
And what is it to cease breathing but to free the breath
    from its restless tides, that it may rise and expand and
    seek God unencumbered?
Only when you drink from the river of silence shall you
    indeed sing.

And when you have reached the mountain top, then you
shall begin to climb.
And when the earth shall claim your limbs, then shall
you truly dance.

For those who grieve for those who have died in pain, or after
long suffering, the translation of this poem by Lucretius is
often most comforting:

From On Life and Death [FR 5]

Departed Comrade! Thou, redeemed from pain,
Shalt sleep the sleep that kings desire in vain:
Not thine the sense of loss
But lo, for us the void
That never shall be filled again.
Not thine, but ours, the grief.
All pain is fled from thee
And we are weeping in thy stead;
Tears for the mourners who are left behind
Peace everlasting for the quiet dead.

I was asked to officiate at the funeral of a man who had committed suicide. His favourite passage was from Shakespeare's
Hamlet, always an appropriate reading for a person who has
committed suicide.

From To Be, or Not to Be [FR 6]

To be, or not to be — that is the question;
Whether 'tis nobler in the mind to suffer
The slings and arrows of outrageous fortune,
Or to take arms against a sea of troubles,
And by opposing end them? To die: to sleep —
No more; and, by a sleep to say we end
The heart-ache and the thousand natural shocks
That flesh is heir to. 'Tis a consummation
Devoutly to be wish'd ...

English literature is immensely rich in all its possibilities.
There are other such readings in the following chapters, and
listed under Bibliography and Further Readings.

MUSIC

Appropriate music is central. One of my most difficult funerals was for a young girl who loved the Spice Girls. At different places in the ceremony we played selections from her favourite songs. At first glance, this may seem frivolous to some people, but I can assure you that it came over as serious and meaningful.

A jazz enthusiast, before he died, left specific instructions for his funeral: a civil celebrant was to perform it, and only a small group of people was to be present; between reflections his favourite music was to be played — selections included 'Muskrat Ramble' and 'Do You Know What It Means to Miss New Orleans'. There was a message in the words of the last song, as we found: the great love of his life was jazz, but the words were 'I miss the ones I care for, more than I miss New Orleans'.

Many funeral directors now have facilities for playing appropriately chosen music. It is always advisable to insist on a rehearsal of the music so that you are assured that the person controlling the music knows how to work the equipment, what the correct volume level should be, and where each selection starts and finishes in the ceremony.

See the suggestions under Music and Songs (pp. 215–16).

SYMBOLS

The use of symbols should be planned in co-operation with a creative funeral director. Common symbols are the national flag draped on the coffin of a returned serviceman; Returned Servicemen's League poppies placed by comrades on the coffin; flowers and decorations of various kinds; a football scarf; badges of office, uniforms, and recognised awards.

Other creative symbolic acts can be obvious. For example, for a librarian who had died, the celebrant and the funeral director arranged for the funeral procession to go to the cemetery past the library where she had contributed so much. The procession stopped there for a few moments, as a mark of respect, before continuing to the burial.

Good funeral celebrants and directors should discuss possibilities of symbols with the bereaved family when they talk over the details of a service.

11 Funeral Ceremonies

A normal funeral ceremony, in my opinion, should never take less than 20 minutes, or go longer than an hour; 25–30 minutes is an acceptable time, given current expectations in our culture.

After the ceremony the celebrant will give the family a printed copy (or recording) of what has been said. This will be kept as a record of our last gesture of regard for the person who has died.

A suggested basic structure for all funeral ceremonies is as follows:

1 Introduction
2 Biography or eulogy
3 Reflection or prayer
4 Readings
5 The committal.

INTRODUCTION

All funeral celebrants have some standard reflections on life and death that are acceptable to most people. In such introductions celebrants should identify themselves, and welcome those who attend.

This can be followed by reflections on the intrusion of

death into our lives, the debt we owe to those who have gone before us, the human instinct to pay tribute, the offering of sympathy to the family, the stimulus we now have to put our values on human relationships and life into perspective, and so on.

Introductions, though general, should not become stereotyped, but should be modified to suit the general tone of the eulogy and the assembled people.

BIOGRAPHY OR EULOGY

Without question, this is the most important part of the ceremony.

The celebrant must visit the family, and, if possible, talk to at least three people. It is helpful to work from ordered questions such as in the list below. The discussion about the person who has died usually takes one to two hours.

The creative and demanding work of writing the biography or eulogy should be done as soon as possible afterwards while the discussion is still fresh. When the eulogy is completed, the celebrant must read it to the family to check for accuracy.

A member of the family, or a family friend, may prefer to write the biography, but the others in the family and the celebrant should also read it well before the ceremony.

A comprehensive ceremony and biography or eulogy should record the following:

For organisation
- The deceased person's full name
- The given name or nickname by which the person was commonly known
- Age
- Date of birth, and date of death
- Contact name (with telephone number)
- Next of kin, or executor of the estate
- Funeral directors (name of contact person, and telephone number)
- Date, time and place of funeral.

The biography/eulogy

- Birthplace; names of parents and siblings
- Early life; primary school
- Teens; secondary school
- Qualifications
- Trade or profession
- Marriage
- Children
- Family life
- Personality
- Community service
- Achievements
- Political ideals
- Hobbies
- Love of nature or animals
- Interests in music, the arts, literature
- Quotations this person liked
- Any other relevant information.

Usually the celebrant composes and delivers the eulogy on behalf of everyone concerned. Naturally, any number of people can participate in the eulogy, but this opportunity is fraught with difficulties. Unless participants are very disciplined and well prepared, they tend to go over time and can cause great distress to grieving relatives. I was once at a state funeral where there were four participants in the eulogy. Each agreed to strictly abide to a five-minute maximum. Three went for five minutes, the last blowhard went for thirty-five minutes. The whole thing got out of hand, and upset everyone present.

'We should only speak good of the dead' — I have always known, and now realise more than ever, that there is some good in everyone. Though sometimes there is a problem in writing a eulogy when the person who has died was not very well liked, there are very few people who have not contributed to humankind in some way, and there is usually something good to say. Sometimes the seemingly ordinary and humble have done a great deal for humanity and/or their family. I have rarely found it difficult to talk about a person in good terms, without exaggeration, excessive praise or presenting an unbalanced picture.

REFLECTION OR PRAYER

Though most funerals by funeral celebrants will be for people who are neither religious nor churchgoers, there are many people who have a general religious belief. In any case there is hardly ever a funeral assembly that does not include both believers and unbelievers.

For this reason most families agree to an optional time of silence in which those who wish to do so may simply reflect or pray according to their wishes, as in the following example ceremonies. During the time of silence appropriate music should be played.

READINGS

Selected texts may be read by the celebrant or readers, with one- or two-sentence introductions as to why the texts have been chosen or why they are considered appropriate. Carefully chosen, such readings can be very meaningful. Selected texts can also be part of the biography or eulogy.

There is no reason why classic religious readings such as 'The Lord's Prayer' or 'The Lord Is My Shepherd', should not be included for the reasons given above, or simply because of their general value in the culture as works of literary beauty.

When the funeral service takes place in one venue, one or two readings are usually enough. When the ceremony is divided, say, between the parlour chapel and the crematorium, the first part of the ceremony finishes with one reading; the final part of the ceremony at the crematorium could begin with one or two readings, followed by the committal.

DIFFERENT VENUES

The main part of the ceremony may be held in a chapel or a funeral parlour, with a final few minutes at a crematorium or graveside; the celebrant simply announces at a natural dividing point that the ceremony will continue at such and such a place. Sometimes the whole ceremony takes place at the crematorium or cemetery.

Funeral ceremonies can be held anywhere — in homes, parks or gardens, or in any place special to the person who has died. I once officiated on a football field for the funeral for a footballer.

THE COMMITTAL

Chosen words are said when the coffin is lowered into the crematorium chamber or the grave. Though couched in a conventional mode, these words can be personalised by referring to the main qualities of the deceased. People usually stand for the final words of the committal on the invitation of the celebrant.

★

There are five different funeral ceremonies in this chapter. They are of actual funerals, though details have been changed to protect privacy; they are reproduced in this way with permission.

Ceremony 1: *Henry Fontaine* (aged 90)

Selected taped music is played before the ceremony.

INTRODUCTION   [FI 1]

Celebrant: My name is Dally Messenger, and I am a civil celebrant. On behalf of the family of Henry Fontaine I thank everyone for coming to this ceremony today.

The memory of the friends who stood by them during this time will be a consolation to them later during those inevitable moments of grief and emptiness.

In a number of ways death unites us all. Henry's death, for a time, demands that each of us put aside our toil, our cares, our business, our pleasure, perhaps even our folly, to unite ourselves with everyone else here, fellow-mourners who share in the common bond of love and respect for Henry. It is at a time like this that we stop the onrush of life, pause for a little while, and reflect. When we think about Henry's life there is quite a lot to reflect upon.

Henry was a unique character. Today you recall the experiences, the relationship, you shared with Henry. As we celebrate his life today you can take satisfaction that Henry has been, and still is, a part of your life. His influence endures, and will continue to endure in the unending consequences flowing from his character and deeds.

BIOGRAPHY/EULOGY [FB 1]

Celebrant: Henry Fontaine was welcomed into the world at Yarrawonga, on the Murray River, on 20 August 1908.

As Eleanor, Eric and I were talking about Henry, we reflected on how his life embraced unquestionably the most interesting period in the world's history. And it is not as though any of this passed Henry by. If anything characterises Henry it was that he was interested in life, the enormous social upheavals, the great discoveries, the marvellous inventions, the momentous political and religious movements of the world that touched his life and formed his character, his values and his approach to living.

I am jumping ahead of myself here, but we all had a laugh when we discussed Henry's home at Glen Iris. In some aspects it looked like that of the legendary Steptoe and Son. He was a hoarder *par excellence*. Anything that might have had any value was kept and hoarded. I know what that is about. Henry was a young man during the Great Depression. The average workingman had nothing, and every purchase was a difficult decision. If you had a job you were lucky, and, strangely, just like it is for many people today, life was precarious, financially precarious. The great horror was waste. Henry lived through two world wars. After the war the man of the house, who invariably built his own home, had to wait years for building materials, tools, even basic equipment. So bits and pieces were precious. Nothing like wood or nails or tiles could ever be thrown out after you lived through that period.

But back to Yarrawonga in 1908. In those days people believed children came cheaper by the dozen — there was actually a book (and later a film) with that title. Henry Junior was the ninth of twelve children. He had three brothers and eight sisters. To feed the family Frank and Mabel, his parents, farmed the land, and we think his father owned a small factory in Yarrawonga.

He has, we believe, only one surviving sister, Desma, who lives in Queensland, and is unable to travel to this service today.

When Henry was about four years of age the family moved to Wangaratta. I am indebted to a short biography of Henry written about twelve years ago by a student, Julia Johnson, for relating that Henry, at the age of six, remembers the young men of Wangaratta boarding the train to go off and fight in World War I. As he grew up in 'Wang' he enjoyed bushwalking, fishing and rabbiting in the Warbie Ranges — a renowned haunt of the Kelly Gang.

As was usual in those times Henry attended school until he reached fourteen years of age, in 1922.

On leaving school he joined the Victorian Railways — starting off as a porter, and absorbed the special culture that goes with being a railwayman. My own grandfather was a railway man during the Depression, and the comings and goings of the trains, the daily timetable, and the system and personalities of the railways was as much the stuff of life, as the rising and the setting of the sun and the air we breathe.

Henry travelled around on the railways as a part of its relieving staff. He therefore became familiar with many country towns in Victoria. Keep in mind that only the very rich or special people owned motor vehicles. The railway lines were the arteries, and the railways themselves were the lifeblood of society. There were few roads — only bush tracks to most places.

But young Henry had a great time. These were the days when people socialised at card games and held parties, but most of all they had a weekly dance in the local hall. To learn ballroom dancing was a rite of passage. Henry became an excellent dancer, and was therefore a great success in country social life. To quote Julia, he travelled around 'attending dances and parties, observing ladies in all their finery; long frilly dresses in many glorious colours; and talking to men in their customary white shirts'. (If a man wore a shirt in any colour other than white, he was thought to be a homosexual!)

It was during these years too that Henry decided he must educate himself. He read widely, and took on board the dictum of Francis Bacon (1561–1626) in *Essay: Of Studies*: 'Reading maketh a full man, conference a ready man and writing an exact man'. Henry read authors like Charles Dickens and J. H. Galbraith, the Australians — Henry Lawson, Banjo Patterson and C. J. Dennis — but most of all, as many of you will recall, he learned from 'conference', from the art of conversation. He honed his mind with discussions and debate.

Another value he absorbed was a love of the Australian bush. He would have experienced it himself, and appreciated the immortal words of Banjo Paterson:

> And he sees the vision splendid, of the sunlit plains extended,
> And at night the wondrous glory of the everlasting stars.

No doubt as a reaction to the world wars and the Great Depression, and in tune with so many working railwaymen, he was touched by Communism. He adopted a great deal of the philosophy of Karl Marx, and, although he was never a card-carrying member of the Communist Party, he certainly was what was called by the communists a 'fellow-traveller'.

In the midst of all this and, somewhere along the line (and I use this cliché advisedly), he met, fell in love with and courted Ivy Adams, an attractive young lady from a distinguished family of Stawell. He was twenty-seven when, in October 1935, they married in the Anglican Church at Stawell. This meant an end to all those parties and dances as a free man — marriage meant the stable life. So Henry settled into the railway signal boxes of Melbourne.

Unusual for those times, children did not quickly follow the marriage. In fact, it wasn't until 2 August 1943 that their first and only child, their daughter Eleanor, was born.

But I am ahead of myself. In 1939 World War II broke out, and Henry, like nearly every young man of his generation, was enthusiastic about signing up for the services. By this time he was quite well qualified in the railway system, and by dint of much study he had qualified as a First Class A Grade Signalman. In short, he was too valuable to send to war (he was classed as having a valued skill in an essential service) so he was not allowed to sign on. Henry took an intense interest in the war, as he did in everything.

Eleanor remembers a very happy childhood with her mother and father. In the years after the war she remembers her excitement when she heard her father come home from his various shifts, and the happy loving years her father and mother had together.

In 1951, at the age of forty-three, Henry had a rush of blood to the head, and decided to leave the railways and 'become his own boss'. He went into various businesses. Eleanor remembers a milk bar in Richmond, a drycleaning business, a taxi-truck. Anyone who is in business for themselves knows that once one gets into that stream one doesn't have much time for anything else.

But, although he was in business, Henry always had the emotional attachment to the trains. (Before I proceed further, in that context I can reflect that our government is going to privatise the trains shortly; I suppose an old Commo like Henry got out just in time!)

Ivy supported Henry in his businesses, but from the early sixties her life took sad turn for the worse. In this last decade of her life she had to struggle with a series of physical illnesses that affected her emotionally and mentally. Henry stood by her during these years, handling the problems as best he could. This was the time, when Ivy worked at Universal Records that they bought the house in Glen Iris. A victim of breast cancer, Ivy died twenty-five years ago.

Henry went into business selling shop supplies and equipment, and in the last years of his life specialised in buying and selling commercial slicers.

He lived life to the full — independently, socially and commercially, until he became ill about two months ago. He died in the Box Hill Hospital last Thursday, 31 July. His daughter Eleanor is a bit put out that Henry didn't stick around for her birthday, but I am sure he did his best!

You look at a photo of Henry Fontaine, and you see a man full of presence and character.

I've mentioned in context the great upheavals, as we could call them, and the great social and political movements, but, when one thinks about it, his life spanned the sensationally interesting developments from the first halting flight of the Wright Brothers to the advent of commercial jumbo jets, man's flight to the moon, and even our vicarious presence on Mars.

During his lifetime he saw the development of radio, television and communication equipment. On my belt is a mobile phone on which anyone can ring me from anywhere in the world at any time. Around Henry were phones and faxes, mobiles and satellite phones. In my office Henry would have engaged me in conversation about e-mail and the Internet. He marvelled at computers, and predicted accurately that they would lead to unemployment.

I must say a few more things for the record so that this tribute is not too incomplete. Henry did not believe in God or religion. He took on board Marx's dictum that it was the 'opiate of the masses', and he couldn't understand how the theory of a good God squared with the horror of the Holocaust, and events like it that we still learn about on an almost daily basis. He felt that if God existed he had a lot to answer for.

Yet he was a totally ethical man in business, completely honest and trustworthy, and upright in his daily life. Eric and I agreed he was a cultural Christian, in the sense that he kept the good values and standards that he had inherited from his Christian past, and he lived by these.

He continued the habit of reading all his life and, strangely for a socialist, loved America — always harbouring a secret desire to visit Harlem in New York. He enjoyed a social drink of wine or beer, but a memory you will have of him is that he loved his cup of tea, a beverage he drank many times a day.

I seem to be implying that he had no blind faith, but that

is not quite correct. He was fanatical devotee of the Richmond Football Club, a Tiger to the core, and if ever there was
a religion in a city with all its symbols, hymns and rituals,
Melbourne has it to the full, and Henry was part of it.

I must mention, too, the wonderful time Henry had as a
devoted member of Parents Without Partners. Although he
generally avoided small talk, and was a bit of male chauvinist,
his was a most pleasant sociable personality, As I mentioned
before, he was superbly skilled ballroom dancer, he liked
people, and thus he made many friends. PWP hosted a memorable 80th birthday party for him at the Lyceum Hall in
Eltham.

It was here that he found an opportunity for the stimulating and challenging conversation so central to his enjoyment
of life. There are many more things I could say about his rich
and interesting life, but time on these occasions is somewhat
limited.

The most important value in life is our relationships. What
goes on the record is that Henry was a devoted husband to his
wife Ivy. Henry was not brought up in an age of, nor was he
attuned to, demonstrating affection and reassurances of love.
In his era you showed love by deeds, by devotion to providing
for one's family, and in other practical ways.

Eleanor loved her father, and was deeply loved in turn by
him. As I said, she has happy memories of her young life, especially treats from her father's milk bar. She was always
conscious that her father was always there — someone on
whom she could always absolutely rely. Eleanor remembers
her father's loving solicitude when she was very ill, and his
pride when she qualified as an accountant, and when she
graduated from university with her Bachelor of Arts degree.

Henry was always happy about Eleanor's marriage to Eric.
The two men grew in respect and affection over the years. The
friendship was forged in the furnace of much forceful and
sometimes artificially-charged discussion. Henry related well
to Eric's parents, Kay and Des, with whom he liked to discuss
the war and other topics of mutual interest.

In the same way Melissa knew she had a grandfather, a bit
of an eccentric perhaps, but a loving grandfather just the same.

Those of you who knew him as a friend knew you were respected and appreciated.

With the passing of Henry Fontaine, a fascinating page of history has closed. The lives of all those who loved, liked and respected him, or related to him at any level, must be diminished.

REFLECTION/PRAYER [FRP 1]

Celebrant: We can take one small consolation from Henry's death — ninety years is a good innings.

Though not a believer, Henry did respect the beliefs of others. So I will now call on everyone to observe a few moments' silence. Those of you who are believers may care to take this opportunity to pray; those of you who are not believers may care to take this time to reflect on the meaning Henry's life had for you.

READING

Celebrant: Finally, I would like to reflect, with some poetic words adapted from Ralph Waldo Emerson, as a tribute to Henry's life of love and achievement.

Adapted from That Man Is a Success [FR 7]

That man is a success
who has lived well,
laughed often and loved much;
who has gained the respect of intelligent men and women
and the love of children;
who has filled his niche and accomplished his task;
who leaves the world better than he found it,
who has never lacked appreciation of Earth's beauty
or failed to express it;
who looked for the best in others,
and gave the best he had.

THE COMMITTAL [FC 1]

Celebrant: As you know, Henry will be privately cremated later, so I will say the words of committal now.

Shortly we will tenderly and reverently commit the body of our friend Henry to the purifying elements, grateful for the life that has been lived, and for all that life has meant to us.

We are glad that Henry lived.
We are glad that we saw his face
and felt the pressure of his hand.
We cherish the memory of his words,
and deeds and character.
We cherish the memory of his family life,
his concern and care,
his vitality and involvement,
especially in conversation,
of his loyalty to his friends.
His place in history.
We cherish his friendship
and, most of all, his love.

We should resolve at moments like these
that while we live we will strive to make our living too
　　of real worth
and carry on Henry's goodness to others.

In the consciousness of work well done
and a life well lived,
death in the deepest sense can have no sting.
We now leave Henry in peace.

Thus thinking of him,
let us leave this place in quietness of spirit,
conscious of the things that really matter in life,
and resolved to live this way toward each other.

Ceremony 2: *Alfred Langworthy (a Buddhist)*

Alfred Langworthy was a man born into Western culture but who later embraced Buddhism. There was no available Buddhist priest to officiate at his funeral, so a civil celebrant was asked to conduct the funeral service. Many of those who attended this funeral were Christians.

A statue of the Buddha was placed on a table, and incense was burnt during the ceremony.

INTRODUCTION [FR 2]

Celebrant: Buddha was born at Kapilavastu, in what is now Nepal, about 563 BC. His father was a chief or Rajah, a member of the Sakya clan. As a youth he became troubled over the sorrows connected with human life. When he grew to young manhood, he felt a deep desire to help people, and to save them from their mental as well as their physical troubles. At the age of twenty-nine he gave up his palace and his inheritance to search for the truth that would bring peace.

It was under the famous Bo Tree that what he considered to be the truth came to his mind. It was then that he was called Buddha, a word that means to become enlightened, or to be wise. Buddha believed that suffering plays a great role in existence. This was the first of the four Noble Truths, which were central to his teaching.

The second truth was that suffering is caused by the desire for pleasure. We are sad because we thirst for things and finally become slaves of things. Desire for possessions prevents us from attaining knowledge and insight. Only the desire for goodness, truth, and salvation is praiseworthy.

The third truth is that by destroying evil desire we may become free from sorrow. Since we have the freedom to make our own choices, we can escape from this bondage whenever we will.

The fourth truth consists of the Noble Eightfold Path that

leads to the end of suffering. It shows how to overcome self-ishness and sorrow, and gain perfect freedom and peace. Buddha called this state Nirvana. It was not heaven as Christians generally think of heaven — Nirvana was perfect insight, a quality of mind.

One of the most important virtues in Buddha's teaching was the knowledge of one's self. Ignorance of the self causes self-centredness, desire, and sorrow. The best way to gain such knowledge is through proper conduct. One must practise self-control, humility, generosity and mercy.

An important virtue to Buddha was love. He said that man must 'cultivate a heart of love that knows no anger, that knows no ill will'. He must spend many hours remembering all living beings with thoughts of love. Such love was universal good will. It expressed itself in helpfulness, charity and generosity, to be shown even to those who would not return it. Buddha said, 'Hatred does not cease by hatred at any time; hatred ceases by love'. When someone is wronged he must put aside all resentment and say, 'My mind shall not be disturbed; no angry word shall escape my lips; I will remain kind and friendly, with loving thoughts and no secret spite'.

I now, in this context, wish to reflect in particular on the person we are gathered here today to pay tribute to, a man who was inspired by the Buddha's teaching and who tried to live by it.

BIOGRAPHY/EULOGY   [FB 2]

Alfred John Langworthy, or Alf, as he was known to you, was born in Richmond, Victoria, in 1924. An only son, he grew up in poor and difficult circumstances.

On leaving school at the beginning of World War II he joined the navy. He saw active service, and in a naval battle he was severely wounded by shrapnel, and almost died. Though it is known that he spent some time in the Middle East, he did not discuss the war very much.

After the war he worked on his mother's farm. Shortly after he did one of the postwar servicemen's courses in watch-making and jewellery.

While practising this craft, at about the age of twenty-six he met Joan. Some time later they married — the beginning of a loving and close relationship that lasted until death and, in their belief, to the hereafter.

Two children were born to the marriage: Belinda and Richard. The parents were made closer by their children, and included them strongly in the circle of their own love.

Alf, meanwhile, had gained qualifications in metallurgy, and exercised this trade as a civilian attached to the RAAF — a position he held until his final illness. As part of his job he had to examine metal stress and fatigue in aeroplanes. He was involved, for example, in preliminary examination on the F111. This took him to the United States. Similar work meant trips to England, France and Malaysia.

About two years ago the wife whom he loved so much died — a blow from which Alf never fully recovered.

Three months ago Alf became very ill with lymphoma, a type of cancer of the lymphatic system. Last week he left hospital, but he had been weakened by the disease and the chemotherapy treatment he had to undergo. Lovingly attended by his daughter Belinda and his son-in-law Des, he died last Monday, 7 August.

As a person Alf was a quiet staid man who kept close control of his emotions. He was calm in demeanour, never known to lose his temper or to argue. He did not smoke or drink immoderately, but lived an enclosed, fairly introverted style of life. Yet he was a generous man, indeed over-generous with money and time to his own family and to people in need. Not a social butterfly, he selected his friends very carefully. He was a meditative man, a thinker about the great truths of the human condition, life and death. He attempted to be independent, appeared strong, but of course was emotionally dependent, as most of us are. Above all, however, he was a family man — devoted to his wife, and supportive, encouraging, and generous to his children.

Most of his life style, as you are all aware, derived from his Buddhist beliefs. A man with a propensity toward the Eastern thought pattern from his early youth, Alf embraced a type of Mahayana Buddhism, which influenced his actions. This had its strengthening in the study of Buddhist religion, his association with Buddhist friends, the study of Buddhist art and his own retreats in Buddhist monasteries.

As well as the characteristics I have mentioned, Alf lived a calculatingly simple life. He was consious of the law of karma in that he knew that all his actions, good and bad, have their endless repercussions throughout the universe. He ate simple healthy foods. He did not involve himself in the complications of the surrounding world, but within the orbit of a completely devoted family life he practised mental control, physical exercise and creative artistry.

He meditated, and studied courses in chiropracty, osteopathy, jewellery, watchmaking, radiology, metallurgy, and navigation. He read extensively, not only books on Buddhism and the creative arts' but Kipling and Brunton and 'The Rubaiyat' of Omar Khayyam (see FR 39). He was always exercising his body, and practised karate and judo.

Not only a good handyman about the home, which was his castle as it were, he was also a creative artist. He carved statuettes of the Buddha and other objects; he painted; he restored antiques; and he created settings for jewellery and gems.

He believed in an immortality and reincarnation whereby his wife would be waiting to meet him, to be with him in facing the mysteries of life or lives beyond this one. Though all death is sad, and the loss can never be belittled, two thoughts about Alf must console us. The first is that Alf's death is a release from pain and suffering — a suffering made more intense because it came on a comparatively young and active man who enjoyed his activity. To symbolise this I have chosen a famous poem of Lucretius, 'On Life and Death' (see FR 5).

It is believed by many that nature does nothing in vain. Alf believed that death is only a type of change.

Alf contributed a great deal to life by the work that he did for his family and for the community, in the war, at Prouds the Jewellers, and in the RAAF.

THE COMMITTAL

Celebrant:

Tenderly and reverently,
we commit the body of Alf to the purifying fire,
grateful for the life that has been lived
and for all that life has meant to us.
We are grateful for the effects
which, according to the law of karma,
came from his goodness to us:

his right belief,
his right aspiration,
his right speech,
his right action,
his right livelihood,
his right effort,
his right thought,
his right meditation.

So we, too, should resolve that, while we live,
we will strive to make our living too of real worth
and carry to others the goodness Alf believed in.

Thus thinking of him,
let us leave this place in quietness of spirit,
conscious of Alf's love and friendship to us,
and determined to live this way toward each other.

Ceremony 3: *Jasmin Reilly* (23, suicide)

(Celebrant, Marjorie Messenger)
This is an abbreviated version.

READING (optional)

Heartache [FR 8]

The hurt is almost unbearable —
yet we will live through it.
It is because we now feel such deep pain,

it is because the inner ache is so great,
that we realise how much we loved her.
And yet the agony inside
gives us a strange comfort.
It tells us how much we loved her.
We really would not want to feel any other way —
Because the grief and heartache we feel
bears witness to the depth of our love.
We know that thoughts of her
will ever bring us comfort.

Dally Messenger

INTRODUCTION   [FR 3]

Celebrant: Ladies and Gentlemen,
My name is Marjorie Messenger, and I am a civil celebrant.
On behalf of the family of Jasmin, or Jas, as some of you knew
her, I thank you for coming to this ceremony today.

'I seem to be drowning in my own thoughts', Jasmin
wrote to her family. I'm sure that we who have gathered here
today to celebrate Jasmin's life, and to farewell her, feel a bit
like that. Our thoughts whirling, confused and questioning as
to why such a young, beautiful, talented and creative girl such
as Jasmin felt so entrapped and overwhelmed by forces outside her control, that she would feel the only way out was to
leave this world.

Later, Anna, Jasmin's sister, will give us insights from words
written by Jasmin herself, as to what was happening to her and
how she felt she had no choice but to leave us this way. Jasmin
asks for understanding and acceptance of her decision and her
reasons for making that decision.

There was never any intention on Jasmin's part to cause
grief to anyone she loved, although she knew her loved ones
would grieve for her. She wrote at length to her family to
reassure them and absolve them from any sense of guilt or
responsibility. Yet one so young cannot know that there is no
escaping the depth of grief experienced when a young one
dies. We grieve most for the passing of the young. This grief is
as much a part of the human condition as love. Those who

love deeply will grieve deeply, no philosophy or religion ever taught can prevent this wholly natural reaction of the human heart.

But when love is unconditional, acceptance and letting go of those we love is equally a part of our human condition. Nothing can now detract from the joy and beauty that you shared with Jasmin; nothing can possibly affect the happiness and depth of experience she herself knew. What has been, has been — forever. The past with all its meaning is sacred and secure. Your love for her and her love for you, her family and friends, cannot now be altered by time or circumstance. You will remember her as a living, vital presence.

As we talk about Jasmin today and in the days and years to come, we will reminisce, and laugh and cry. Eventually the times we grieve will grow further apart and shorter of duration, while our fears we might forget her will dissipate. Our memories of her will grow stronger. And is it not true that our lives from one moment to the next, become, simply, memories?

BIOGRAPHY/EULOGY [FB 3]

Celebrant: Jasmin was born on 15 July 1975. 'What a pretty baby!' passers-by used to say as she was wheeled down the street. A pretty baby and toddler she was, but Jasmin was also quick to learn and comprehend the world around her. She rapidly learnt to speak, perhaps a very early indication of the talent for creative writing that was to emerge as she grew up. At thirteen, Jasmin wrote a poem about a seal, which Anna will read.

As a little girl, Jasmin loved playing fun word-games with her dad. When Ray was suffering from back and neck pain, Jasmin said to him, 'When you get those pains I'm afraid you're going to be sterilised'. When she saw the look on everyone's faces she added, 'What's the word I'm after?' (Of course, she meant paralysed!) When Jasmin learnt about dinosaurs in primary school she asked her dad, 'Were there still dinosaurs around when you were a little boy, Dad?'

Jasmin was a good scholar, and she never made a spelling

mistake. She was not only a creative writer but was also very creative in other ways too — at a very young age she made lavender bags for her family and friends.

School brought out the academic side of Jasmin more than the creative, and in sixth grade Ray found himself compere at a school concert where the boy and girl winners of the annual top award, the award for duxes of the school, were announced. He was surprised and delighted to hear his own daughter's name being read out.

During her primary school years Jasmin developed many of her creative talents. She went to a music school; learnt swimming in Malvern; joined a gymnastics club; took horseriding lessons; learnt piano from Vivienne Stewart, completing her grade five exam; and took ballet lessons from the Prahran Ballet School, where the principal commented to Ray, 'Jasmin is good at her work because she thinks'.

After completing her VCE year at secondary school, Jasmin went to France, as an exchange student. She was only there for three months, yet found herself thinking in French. She came home speaking the language fluently.

She then went on to the University of Melbourne to study economics. However, she found she excelled in the arts side of the course, so she changed direction and finished her Arts degree at La Trobe University.

Attending university gave Jasmin a lot more confidence, and improved her social skills — from a young child she had been rather shy.

After completing her degree Jasmin had a year off before starting a professional creative writing course at Monash University. During her time off, she moved out of home and enjoyed the freedom of being out on her own. She worked casually, and had a fun-filled social life. She learnt a lot about the Aquarian Age, and this knowledge gave her some comfort, for she felt at home with the philosophies embodied within it.

Jasmin, I'm told, was a perfectionist. It became a joke amongst the family that one had only to receive and try to undo the sticky tape binding the wrapper around a carefully and expertly packaged gift from her, to know that everything had to be perfectly done.

She met her best friend, Carla, in primary school, and while they did not always keep in touch they were still the best of friends. Carla had a good sense of humour, and she and Anna and Jas often sat around the table, giggling and laughing at nothing in particular — just enjoying each other's company.

Love flowed to Jasmin, and from her. After looking at a photograph of her and learning about her, I can see why.

REFLECTION/PRAYER [FRP 2]

Celebrant: Sadly, after reading her words, I can also see and understand why she left us. Ariel, the mother she loved so much, will tell us now, a little about the why.

Simone, too, would like to say a few words about her friend. Then Jim, Jasmin's boyfriend, will finish our reflections on Jasmin's life.

Ariel, Simone and Jim all speak in turn.

We will now pause for a moment's reflection: for some a time for prayer, for all of us a time to reflect on the meaning Jasmin's life had for us. While we do, Anna is going to sing Ben Harper's 'Waiting for an Angel'.

In one of the letters Jasmin wrote one night when her thoughts overwhelmed her and she was fearing for her sanity, she went outside and sat on the grass in the dark to try to bring herself back to a sense of reality.

Nature is one reality we all share. And it seems to me that Jasmin sensed that connecting with the earth, as Ariel said, the sky and the darkness created by nature is protective rather than threatening. In this sense, the darkness enveloping Jasmin's mind, would bring some sense of connecting to that which is real. Sadly, unable to ground herself through nature, Jasmin, with love, took full responsibility for her own actions.

THE COMMITTAL [FC 3]

Celebrant: Please stand for the words of the committal.

Jasmin's ashes will be scattered over the gentle earth
that has been the chief supporter of humans
since we first walked beneath the sun.
To all human beings, to all living forms,
the soil has ever provided the sustenance
that is the stuff of life.

To that good earth, Jasmin's ashes will be committed,
and we can say with the poet Shelley:

From Adonais [FR 9]

She is made one with Nature: there is heard
Her voice in all of nature's music, from the moan
Of thunder, to the song of night's sweet bird;
She is a presence to be felt and known
In darkness and in light, from herb and stone, ...

She is a portion of the loveliness
Which once she made more lovely ...

Ceremony 4: Sarah Hammond (12, traffic accident)

INTRODUCTION [FC 4]

Celebrant: On behalf of the parents and the family of Sarah Hammond, I thank everyone for coming to this ceremony today.

Death in a number of ways unites us all. This young girl's death, for a time, demands that each one of us put aside our toil, our cares, our business, our pleasure and our folly, to unite ourselves with everyone here as fellow-mourners who share in the common bond of love for Sarah.

We grieve most for the passing of the young. If the old depart we recognise a natural change, as when the sunset dissolves naturally into the dusk and the stars come out in the night. But the death of youth shocks us as if the morning were suddenly overcast by blackness — the day suffering a dreadful eclipse.

This very grief is a token that death cannot take from us the most precious of our treasures — namely, love. It is the tear of love that flows the fullest, the pain of love that aches the deepest, the thoughts of love that move us most profoundly. Other passions have their tears and pains; but none are so keen in their sense of loss as love is. For love is of the very essence of the human heart; and, when we are deprived of the child we love, our inner soul seems rent in two, and life is only a part of what it was.

The intense feeling of love that grieves for the young shows that nature itself is teaching us to keep hold of something that is truly worth keeping. Of all memories, the memory of the young moves us more deeply than any other.

The memory of Sarah will bring refreshment to our hearts and strengthen and comfort us. We shall remember her as a living vital presence.

I think we can take comfort, too, from the reflection that nothing can now detract from the love and closeness that you shared with Sarah, nothing can possibly affect the happiness and shared life that you had with her. What has been, has been, forever. The past with all its meaning and beauty is sacred and secure. Our love for her and her love for us cannot be altered by time or circumstance.

BIOGRAPHY/EULOGY (abbreviated)   [FB 4]

Celebrant: Sarah lived her short life in Clayton, and was a pupil at the Clayton State School until her tragic death last Saturday.

As a baby and a young girl she had to face many difficulties. She was assisted by loving parents, her brother and her sisters, through a great deal of sickness and emotional trouble. She suffered, for example, from asthma and eye trouble and all the difficulties in relating to people that such handicaps involve. In short, for most of her brief life she was a struggler. I think it was a tribute to Sarah herself and to her parents that in a painstaking way she overcame her problems and developed into a beautiful young girl.

In the last two or three years her ability to give affection and relate to her father and mother, her brother and sisters, and her close friends developed and blossomed.

She was a quiet, non-aggressive girl who nevertheless loved life. She formed very close relationships with her sister Julia and some of her school friends.

When I spoke to her teacher yesterday, it came home strongly to me that she was liked by all her school friends who enjoyed her pleasant company.

She shared with her friends an interest in the world around her, an enjoyment of TV programmes like 'The Simpsons' and 'Home and Away', and in fantasies of science fiction like 'Star Wars'.

There are a number of other things I could mention but the interest that most stands out was her passion for the music of the pop singer Natalie Imbruglia. Because Sarah loved this music and it was such a love of her life, I will play selections of this music to bring out one aspect of Sarah's character.

Sarah was an intensely personal girl. The best illustration I have of this is her practice on birthdays and at Christmas of drawing and sketching her own cards as presents.

Though not demonstrative by nature, Sarah did love and trust people. She felt a deep sympathy for anyone in pain or trouble. In part of the song I will now play for our reflection, the lyrics point out that people need hope, love and trust. I think, as we play this song, one of the tributes we can pay to Sarah's memory is to love and trust each other more.

REFLECTION/PRAYER   [FRP 3]

Celebrant: To the immediate family, to her parents, Des and Claudia, to Debbie, David and Julia, we all extend our deepest sympathy. We come with them as mourners: we share their grief. When at other times we grieve — over lost opportunities, lost wealth or our health — whenever a loss brings sorrow it is our part to turn the affliction to some wise purpose in our life's experience.

The reflection I must now make to everyone present is an obvious one. Each of us here must bring ourselves to do something about, and campaign for, the avoidance of the sort of tragedy that ended our beautiful Sarah's life and the lives of so many others.

I will conclude this part of the ceremony by playing Sarah's favourite song. During this time we can reflect on the meaning Sarah's life had for us.

After this part of the service we will proceed to the Chapel at the Crematorium.

★

The ceremony then continued at the Crematorium, beginning with the reading of 'Heartache' (see FR8).

THE COMMITTAL [FC 4]

Celebrant:

Before we commit the body of Sarah,
let us be thankful for the intangibles:
the impact of her life on ours;
we remember her smile, her frown, her quizzical look;
her courage in the face of adversity;
her sympathy; her love of life;
The significant moments and the fun times we had with
    her;
the times we struggled with her and searched with her.
But most of all we will remember her love
for as long as we live.

Tenderly and reverently,
we commit the body of Sarah to the purifying fire,
grateful for the life that has been lived;
for all that her life has meant to us.
We are glad that she lived.
We are glad that we saw her face,
and felt the pressure of her hand.
We cherish the memory of her words and deeds,
and her character.
We cherish her friendship.

In token of our love for the young life
that has untimely ended,
let us resolve to offer a more generous affection
to each other,
as far as we are able,
and to young children the world over.

We leave her in peace, and bid her farewell.

Ceremony 5: *Rebecca Toon* (baby, sudden death)

(Celebrant, Marjorie Messenger)

Author's note: In these heartrending circumstances it is helpful to make full use of personal symbols, e.g. a teddy bear, toys, candles, balloons, or similar objects.

INTRODUCTION   [FI 5]
Celebrant:

There are no words of comfort that can cushion the shock experienced when one is faced with sudden and unexpected death. Even more so when that death is the death of a baby. There does not seem to be any point in searching for meaning and sense, rhyme or reason, in such a death. Rather one feels anger and pain and hurt, and deep, deep sorrow that such a thing as this can happen.

Yet, there is one thing that can never be taken away, and that is the experience of loving and having been loved. Love flowed from the hearts of those who surrounded and were close to Rebecca, and she responded to this love.

BIOGRAPHY/EULOGY (abbreviated)   [FB 5]
Celebrant: Rebecca was a loving baby, with a happy disposition. Although she was born a little prematurely and weighed

only 2.3 kg at birth, once she left the hospital she grew into a healthy baby who did not suffer any sickness.

Rebecca was a much-loved baby. She was a fortunate little girl who was surrounded by a large and loving family. Her mother Lyn, and her father John; her grandmother Catherine, six doting uncles and two aunties.

Rebecca was very much the centre of attention and there was never a shortage of babysitters. The boys loved to play with her, and she knew how to play up to them, to be picked up, cuddled and played games with. Rebecca was sure of the love that was given freely to her by so many. Secure in this love, she was able to grow and relate to others with confidence and cheeky assurance. Not all babies have such love surrounding them. Rebecca was one of the lucky ones.

A void is left, an emptiness, with her going. Only time can ease and dull the heartache felt by those who loved Rebecca. You who loved her are left with a legacy of beautiful and happy memories. I feel the words of the following poem express well what we are faced with when a loved one dies and we have to carry on with the daily routine of living.

READING

You're Gone [FR 10]

The time has come and now we part,
Thoughts of you so close to my heart,
The loss is like a burning pain,
I would give it all, to see you again.

But no, you're gone. In time I know
The pain will fade away,
The thoughts and memories will still be there,
In my heart you'll always stay.

Janice G. Jenkin

REFLECTION/PRAYER [FRP 4]

Celebrant: I now ask everyone to observe a minute's silence. Those of us who are believers may care to take this opportunity to pray; those of us who are not believers may care to take this time to reflect on the meaning Rebecca's life had for us.

If appropriate, reflections similar to the introduction to *Sarah Hammond*'s funeral (see Ceremony 4) could be given here.

READINGS

Her Role Down Here Is Done [FR 11]

Her little soul has touched us all,
She didn't need to stay:
Her spirit touched each one of us
Before it sailed away.

We all know souls arrive on earth
With special roles to fill,
And hers has fully played its part,
Her memory guides us still.

She had a very special soul
She stayed but just a while;
So if, or when, you're feeling sad
Recall her with a smile.

For then you'll know inside your heart
The reason why she's gone;
And never feel too empty that
Her role down here is done.
Her spirit touched each one of us,
No other ever could.
Forever will we cherish her
The way we know we should!

THE COMMITTAL [FC 5]

Celebrant:

Tenderly and reverently,
we commit the body of this little one to the elements,
and ultimately to Mother Earth from which all life comes,
and to which, in the end, all life returns.

We are glad that Rebecca lived.
We are glad that we saw her face
and felt the touch of her hand.
We cherish the memory of her first smile,
her first tooth,
her happy disposition.
We cherish the memory of the joy
and beauty she brought to us.

We grieve that she never reached her potential.
We take joy in that she brought so much love and
    meaning into our lives.
We will remember her for the rest of our lives.
We sadly bid her farewell.

12 Alternatives (for Funerals)

Introduction

AGNES* (aged 85)   [FI 6]

(Celebrant, Kathy Hurley)

Celebrant: We are gathered here today in remembrance of a special person in our lives, and in doing so we are all aware that our lives are interrelated and composed of many facets from birth until the final time of death. Our being here today is yet another — a meaningful experience of love and friendship for *Agnes* and her family, and on their behalf I thank you for being here with them to celebrate *Agnes*'s life and to say goodbye to her in a loving and meaningful way.

The event of death has a way of uniting us in a way that perhaps no other human experience does. It reminds us of the fragility of our relationships; it reminds us of the special and unique way in which we relate to those people who cross our pathways in life.

It is at a time like this that we think, too, of the great debt

---

*In all ceremonies substitute your own names and the names of the other people involved for the names in italics.

we owe to the past — to all the men and women who have gone before us, and how each of them have contributed something, great or small, to the benefit of mankind as a whole. Their work has not only benefited others in their own time, but also future generations.

It is often said when those who were very old die, 'They had a good innings'. This may be comforting for some people, but it does not necessarily make it easier to accept the loss of an aged relative. Very old people are a special part of the family tree. They provide a link with our past and with the past of our parents, our uncles and aunts and our grandparents — people we may never have known. They represent the history and survival of our family and provide a feeling of permanence in a changing world.

I believe that reflecting on our past and our history brings knowledge, comfort and a sense of identity and psychological balance. Though this is a very sad occasion, in it there can also be a depth of joy that brings wisdom and strength.

Let us now turn now to remember with love and gratitude, the life of our friend *Agnes*. Each of you have your own personal memories, the impact of her life of yours — let me lead your thoughts as we recall her life.

GRACE DAVIES (aged 70) [FI 7]

Celebrant: On behalf of the family of *Grace Davies* I thank everyone for coming to this ceremony today.

Death in a number of ways unites us all. *Grace's* death, for a time demands that each one of us put aside our toil, our cares, our business, our pleasure and our folly, to unite ourselves with everyone here, as fellow-mourners who share in the common bond of love and respect for *Grace*.

It is fitting that we should reflect on what we owe to those who have gone before us. Our lives are but the latest notes in a music that began with the birth of humanity itself. That music is a song of households knit in the bonds of mutual affection; of cities and states built up by courage and self-devotion; of benefits bestowed by wit and labour — not only for the aid of the weak and helpless, but for the benefit of all;

of knowledge won from nature; of precious thoughts and teaching imparted by wise men and women through the ages. How immense and how deep is our debt to the past!

How much we owe to the goodness, the intelligence, and the energy of men and women who are now dead, and who toiled in faith and patience for the children of their day, and for us of a remoter time. How few of these forerunners have we known? Yet we derive from them our life, our health, our stores of sustenance, our learning, our all. It is one of our profoundest joys to know that we are united to this great past. As Auguste Comte said, 'To live in thought with the dead is one of the most precious privileges of humanity'.

Biography/Eulogy

DR NEIL SUTHERLAND   [FB 6]
(Celebrant, Kathy Hurley)

Celebrant: Dr Neil Sutherland died quietly on Monday, 13 January, at the nursing home where he had lived for some time. With the tragic onset of Alzheimer's disease, these last years have seen a gradual decline in his health. For him and his family, death has brought a certain release from the difficulties they have faced. For his family, a mixture of emotions: firstly, a certain relief that Neil no longer has to suffer; that the on-going grief at watching his health deteriorate is now over, but at the same time, grief in their loss. No matter how much we want the pain to finish and death to bring peace, we are never really completely prepared for the finality of the separation when a loved one dies. I must say that, through it all, Neil was true to himself.

As always, he did things his way; his will remained strong and, as his family and the nursing staff know, if he'd made up his mind about something, there was no changing it! From the start, he fought this illness, although there was little anyone could do. Even at the end his will was still strong. Neil died in Gill's arms, knowing so much love and care and attention so freely given him by his family and the wonderful staff of the nursing home.

In times of sorrow, as in times of joy, we feel a need to share. Shared laughter heightens our enjoyment, and shared sorrow makes more enduring our comfort. We are here today because we feel a great sense of loss in Neil's death. Today we also find that memories are crowding in on us — living memories that are tokens of a great gift, a life that has been shared.

You are happy that Neil was, and still is, a real part of your lives. The influence of his personality, his character and deeds will live on in your acts and thoughts. You will remember him as a living, vital presence. That memory will bring refreshment to your hearts and strengthen you in times of trouble. These are reflections that you treasure, for there can never be too much friendship in the world, too much generosity or too much love.

ADAM CRUIKSHANK (21, motorbike accident)   [FB 7]
(Celebrant, Marjorie Messenger)

The words I have just read from a John Lennon song reflect very clearly the way Adam felt about society and the world as we know it. He hated institutions and systems, and society as it is organised today. He refused to conform, to compromise his ideals, to sacrifice his individuality and emerging identity to the materialistic world he lived in. Despite the fact that he attended thirteen schools, Adam matriculated — on his own terms — not to gain the highest marks possible but to achieve something he had made up his mind he would achieve. After he left school he worked for a time with CSIRO. However, Adam found the job and the studies involved too restrictive, so he left the job. After that he took on a number of part-time positions working, again, only to achieve the desired goal, and then he would stop and fill his life with his real loves: his girl Lyn; his cat Sylvester, and his beloved motorbike.

Adam lived for his bike. Perhaps it would be more truthful to say he lived for what the bike represented — freedom — the wind in his face, the soaring flying motion of the bike, and the challenge to learn (he was always pulling them apart), to grow, to increase in awareness of life, of himself and of the universe. His thirst for knowledge led him to a deepening and growing awareness of all that he was seeking. Adam was eager to impart his knowledge to others. In fact, he felt led very strongly to do so. He would deliberately provoke friends to stir them up, and get them arguing and thinking. There were a number of things Adam felt very strongly about. He did not smoke or drink or take drugs. He saw these as looking in the wrong direction. He did not believe in wars, feeling that anybody who killed for any reason was, to quote John Lennon, 'crippled inside'. He ate health foods, though occasionally he weakened — as he confessed to his mum one day, 'Mum, I've just eaten eight dim sims'!

Adam had a fine sense of humour, and Spike Milligan's humour appealed to him as the best. He loved music, and John Lennon was a firm favourite. He was a good artist at school, even at sixteen his paintings showed the depth of his thought.

Adam was not religious in the conventional sense, but he believed in a higher spirit or force and he was not afraid to die. He believed in following his own conscience; he lived out the philosophy of 'Here today, gone tomorrow'. He was open to his friends and his family, and he appreciated people revealing their real selves to him. He made friends, for he was a happy-go-lucky person. He was also open to learning — learning something from all with whom he came in contact. Adam, as you all know, was killed in an accident on Friday night while riding his bike. It seems to me that it is fitting that Adam's bike — his symbol of freedom — was instrumental in causing his death, his release into new realms of freedom, knowledge and awareness. As Joan Anglund says, 'There is only one doorway into forever, and Death keeps the only key'.

Reflection/Prayer

VALDA [FRP 5]

Celebrant: I now call on everyone to observe a few minutes' silence. Those of you who are believers may care to take this time to pray; those of you who are not believers may just wish to take this time to reflect on the meaning *Valda*'s life had for you.

To the immediate family — to *Fiona* and *Fred*, *Jean* and *Rex*, and their families — we all extend our deepest sympathy. We come with them as mourners. We share their grief. When at other times we grieve — over lost opportunities, lost wealth or health, whenever a loss brings sorrow it is our part to turn the affliction to some wise purpose in our life's experience. We cannot think of *Valda*'s death without resolving to live a fuller, more meaningful life of our own. Because we loved her, because we are here, even now she exerts her influence on us. Her death causes us to get our values into perspective.

While we sincerely grieve today because we are parting with someone we have known and loved, we are also faced with the fact that we do not mourn alone. At this very moment thousands of others are mourning the loss of their loved ones. Many of these have not died in peace, at the end of a full and useful life as *Valda*'s was. Many have seen their loved ones torn from them by the awful demands of people's inhumanity to others.

Bearing in mind the sorrows that others are experiencing today, we come to realise that we are living in a larger world than our own, and that the best way to face the unavoidable fact of death and parting is to take upon our shoulders the troubles of others, to go on working that we may help to remove the existing causes of injustice and preventable sorrow in this world.

We will now proceed to the Fawkner Crematorium, where the final part of this ceremony will take place.

Readings

Sorrow   [FR 12]

She sought her native land again;
The swallow takes its ragged flight.
We went together day and night
Till parting drew her from my sight,
And tears fell down like rain.

She went her native land to seek,
Now up, now down the swallow flies.
And oh! the last of tender ties,
The form that fades from aching eyes,
And tears come coursing down my cheek.

Around, around, the swallows dart.
She went into her far country,
And when I vainly sought to see
The empty landscape mocked at me,
And great grief settled on my heart.

Ancient Chinese poem

When Death Knocks [FR 13]

On the day when death will knock at thy door,
what wilt thou offer to him?
I will set before my guest the full vessel of my life.
I will never let him go with empty hands.
All the sweet vintage of all my autumn days and summer
   nights,
All the earnings and gleanings of my busy life
will I place before him, at the close of my day.

Rabindranath Tagore

Ecclesiastes 3:1–8 [FR 14]

There is a season for everything,
A time for every occupation under heaven;
A time for giving birth, a time for dying;
A time for planting, a time for uprooting what has been
   planted.
A time for killing, a time for healing;
A time for knocking down, a time for building.
A time for tears, a time for laughter;
A time for mourning, a time for dancing.
A time for throwing stones away, a time for gathering
   them up;
A time for embracing, a time to refrain from embracing.

A time for searching, a time for losing;
A time for keeping, a time for throwing away.
A time for tearing, a time for sewing;
A time for keeping silent, a time for speaking.
A time for loving, a time for hating,
A time for war, a time for peace.

From Break, Break, Break [FR 15]

Break, break, break,
On thy cold gray stones, O Sea!
And I would that my tongue could utter
The thoughts that arise in me

And the stately ships go on
To their haven under the hill;
But O for the touch of a vanish'd hand,
And the sound of a voice that is still.

Alfred, Lord Tennyson

Requiem [FR 16]

Under the wide and starry sky,
Dig the grave and let me lie:
Glad did I live and gladly die,
And I laid me down with a will.
This be the verse you grave for me:
Here he lies where he longed to be;
Home is the sailor, home from the sea,
And the hunter home from the hill.

Robert Louis Stevenson

Away [FR 17]

I cannot say and I will not say
That she is dead — she is just away.
With a cheery smile and a wave of a hand
She has wandered into an unknown land,
And left us dreaming how very fair
It needs must be since she lingers there.

James Whitcomb Riley

From The Tempest [FR 18]

Our revels now are ended. These our actors,
As I foretold you, were all spirits, and
Are melted into air, into thin air;
And, like the baseless fabric of this vision,
The cloud-capp'd towers, the gorgeous palaces,
The solemn temples, the great globe itself,
Yes, all which it inherit, shall dissolve,
And, like the insubstantial pageant faded,
Leave not a rack behind. We are such stuff
As dreams are made on; and our little life
Is rounded with a sleep.

William Shakespeare

From The Book of the Dead [FR 19]

As each day ends may I have lived,
That I may truly say:
I did no harm to human kind,
From truth I did not stray;
I did no wrong with knowing mind,
From evil I did keep;
I turned no hungry person away,
I caused no one to weep.

Ancient Egyptian (c. 4500 BC)

Song [FR 20]

When I am dead, my dearest,
Sing no sad songs for me;
Plant thou no roses at my head,
Nor shady cypress tree:
Be the green grass above me
With showers and dewdrops wet;
And if thou wilt, remember,
And if thou wilt, forget.

I shall not see the shadows,
I shall not feel the rain;
I shall not hear the nightingale
Sing on, as if in pain;
And dreaming through the twilight
That doth not rise nor set,
Haply I may remember,
And haply may forget.

Christina Rossetti

daffodils   [FR 21]

in times of daffodils (who know
the goal of living is to grow)
forgetting why, remember how
in time of lilacs who proclaim
the aim of waking is to dream,
remember so (forgetting seem)

in time of roses (who amaze
our now and here with paradise)
forgetting if, remember yes

in time of all sweet things beyond
whatever mind may comprehend,
remember seek (forgetting find)

and in a mystery to be
(when time from time shall set us free)
forgetting me, remember me

e. e. cummings

The Dead   [FR 22]

These hearts were woven of human joys and cares,
Washed marvellously with sorrow, swift to mirth.
The years had given them kindness. Dawn was theirs,
And sunset, and the colours of the earth.

These had seen movement, and heard music;
Known slumber and waking; loved; gone proudly
    friended;

Felt the quick stir of wonder; sat alone;
Touched flowers and furs and cheeks.

All this is ended.

Rupert Brooke

Memories and Peace   [FR 23]

Why smile in such sadness?
It's because of the memories
of laughter shared in the past.
The humour of life, the fun and the joy,
The reminiscences certain to last.

Why relief in such sadness,
It's because there is peace
With no more chance of pain
No one can hurt, nor take away
There will never be fear again.

Gloria Matthew

Death Is Nothing at All   [FR 24]

Death is nothing at all,
I have only slipped away
into the next room.

I am I, and you are you.
Whatever we were to each other,
that we are still.

Call me by my old familiar name,
speak to me in the easy way
which you have always used.
Put no difference in your tone,
wear no forced air of solemnity or sorrow.

Laugh as we always laughed
at the little jokes we enjoyed together.
Let my name be ever the household word
that it always was,
let it be spoken without effect,
without a trace of a shadow on it.

Life means all that it ever meant.
It is the same as it ever was;
there is unbroken continuity.
Why should I be out of mind
because I am out of sight?
I am waiting for you, for an interval
somewhere very near,
just around the corner.

All is well.

Canon Henry Scott-Holland

Her Old Bones Creaked [FR 25]

Her old bones creaked
And her pace was slow,
But her smile was blindingly bright.
Her mind was sharp
And her voice was kind,
Her manner was a true delight.

The world had changed
In the winters she'd known
But she bore their weight with pride.
She shared her wisdom
And passed the goodness on,
Using her love of life as her guide.

She did not bow to time,
Using life as her stage,
She sought each morning's joy,
And she was never defeated by age.

Jamie Samms

Death of a Baby [FR 26]

I was not aware of the moment when I first crossed the
    threshold of this life.
What was the power that made me open out into this
    vast mystery like a bud in the forest at midnight?

When in the morning I looked upon the light I felt in a
   moment that I was no stranger in this world, that the
   inscrutable without name and form had taken me in
   its arms in the form of my own mother.
Even so, in death the same unknown will appear as ever
   known to me.
And because I love this life, I know I shall love death as
   well.
The child cries out when from the right breast the
   mother takes it away, in the very next moment to
   find in the left one its consolation.

Rabindranath Tagore

Stillborn Child   [FR 27]

I carried you in hope
for many long months,
remembered that close hour
when we made you,
often felt you kick and move
as slowly you grew within me,
wondered what you would look like
when your wet head emerged
girl or boy, and at what glad moment
I should hear your birth cry,
and I welcoming you with all you needed
of warmth and food;
we had a home waiting for you.

After my strong labourings,
sweat cold on my limbs,
my small cries merging
with the summer air,
you came. You did not cry!
You did not breathe,
we had not expected this.
It seems your birth had no meaning,
or had you rejected us?
They will say that you did not live,
register you as stillborn.

But you lived for me all that time
in the dark chamber of my womb,
and when we think of you now,
perfect in your little death,
We know that for us
you are born still;
We shall carry you with us forever,
our child, you were always ours,
you are ours now.
Death and life are the same mysteries.

The Tide Recedes [FR 28]

The tide recedes, but leaves behind
bright seashells on the sand.

The sun goes down but gentle warmth
still lingers on the land.

The music stops and yet it lingers on
in sweet refrain.

For every joy that passes
something beautiful remains.

M. D. Hughes

Mutual Hearts [FR 29]

Mutual hearts are like the flowers
That twine themselves together
When morning sends the drenching showers
Or evening comes to wither.

And though they fall —
As fall they must
They will not, cannot sever
But sink together to the dust
And together lie forever.

Life has changed in many ways
But some things last forever
Like memories of happy times
That we all spent together.

Those Who Love [FR 30]

It's always those who love the most
Who most miss the one they love,
When comes the parting of the ways,
And clouds loom dark above;
But tears will pass, your skies will clear
Then will you smile again,
And comfort find in memories,
Which now bring bitter pain.

The Measure of a Man [FR 31]

Not 'How did he die?' but 'How did he live?'
Not 'What did he gain?' but 'What did he give?'
These are the units of a man, as a man,
To measure the worth, regardless of birth.

Not 'What was his station?' but 'Had he a heart?'
And 'How did he play his own special part?'
'Was he ever ready, with a word of good cheer
To bring back a smile, to banish a tear?'
Not 'What was his church? Nor 'What was his creed?'
But 'Had he defended those really in need?'
Not 'What did the sketch in the newspaper say?'
But 'How many were sorry when he passed away?'

The Day You Left [FR 32]

With tears we saw you suffer,
As we watched you fade away,
Our hearts were almost broken,
As you fought so hard to stay.
We knew you had to leave us,
But you never went alone,
For part of us went with you
The day you left your home.

Yours and Yours and Yours   [FR 33]

The life that I have is all that I have
And the life that I have is yours,
The love that I have of the life that I have
Is yours, and yours, and yours.

A rest I shall have, a sleep I shall have,
Yet Death will be but a pause,
For the peace of my years in the long green grass
Will be yours, and yours, and yours.

One at Rest   [FR 34]

Think of me as one at rest,
for me you should not weep,
I have no pain, no troubled thoughts,
for I am just asleep.
The living thinking me that was,
is now forever still.
And life goes on without me
as time forever will.

If your heart is heavy now
because I've gone away,

Dwell not long upon it, friend,
for none of us can stay.
Those of you who liked me
I sincerely thank you all,
And those of you who loved me
I thank you most of all.

The answer to life's riddle
in life I never knew,
I go with hope that now I will,
and even so will you.
Oh, foolish, foolish me that was,
I who was so small,
To have wondered, even worried,
at the mystery of it all.

And in my fleeting lifespan
as time went rushing by,
I found some time to hesitate,
to laugh, to love, to cry.
Matters it now if time began,
if time will ever cease?
I was here, I used it all,
and now I am at peace.

Farewell to You [FR 35]

Farewell to you,
and the youth I have spent with you.

It was but yesterday we met in a dream,
but let me figure in your daily talk,
tell of my loves and joys,
of how I used to laugh,
that way you will keep me in your memory.

This is my hope of immortality.

I Did Not Die [FR 36]

Do not stand at my grave and weep,
I am not there, I do not sleep.
I am a thousand winds that blow,
I am the diamond glints on snow,
I am the sunlit-ripened grain,
I am the gentle Autumn's rain.

When you awake in the morning hush
I am the swift, uplifting rush
Of quiet birds in circled flight,
I am the stars that shine at night.
Do not stand at my grave and cry,
I am not there. I did not die.

There Is No Death [FR 37]

I am standing on the seashore. A ship at my side spreads
her white sails to the morning breeze and starts for
the blue ocean.

She is an object of beauty and strength and I stand and
watch her until at length she is a speck of white
cloud just where the sea and sky come to mingle
with each other.

Then someone at my side says, 'There, she's gone!'
Gone where? Gone from my sight, that is all. She is just
as large in mast and hull and spar as she was when she
left my side, and she is just as able to bear her load of
living weight to her destined harbour.

Her diminished size is in me, not in her, and just at the
moment when someone at my side says, 'There, she's
gone! there are other eyes watching her coming, and
other voices ready to take up the glad shout, 'Here,
she comes!'

And that is dying.

This Heritage [FR 38]

They are not dead,
who leave us this great heritage
of remembered joy.
They still live in our hearts,
in the happiness we knew,
in the dreams we shared.

They still breathe,
in the lingering fragrance windblown,
from their favourite flowers.
They still smile in the moonlight's silver
and laugh in the sunlight's sparkling gold.

They still speak in the echoes of words
we've heard them say again and again.
They still move,

in the rhythm of waving grasses,
in the dance of the tossing branches.
They are not dead;
their memory is warm in our hearts,
comfort in our sorrow.
They are not apart from us,
but a part of us
For love is eternal,
and those we love shall be with us
throughout all eternity.

The Rubaiyat [FR 39]

Ah, make the most of what we yet may spend,
Before we too into the Dust descend;
Dust into Dust, and under Dust, to lie,
Sans Wine, sans Song, sans Singer, and — sans End!
…
The Moving Finger writes; and, having writ,
Moves on: nor all thy Piety nor Wit
Shall lure it back to cancel half a Line,
Nor all thy Tears wash out a Word of it.

Alas, that Spring, should vanish with the Rose!
That Youth's sweet-scented Manuscript should close!
The Nightingale that in the Branches sang,
Ah, when, and whither flown again, who knows.

Omar Khayyam

Song [FR 40]

Life is ours in vain
Lacking love, which never
Counts the loss or gain.
But remember, ever
Love is linked with pain.

Light and sister shade
Shape each mortal morrow
Seek not to evade
Love's companion Sorrow,
And be not dismayed.

Grief is not in vain,
It's for our completeness.
If the fates ordain
Love to bring life sweetness,
Welcome too its pain.

*Oodgeroo of the tribe Noonuccal
(formerly known as Kath Walker)*

Excerpt from the Curly-Pyjama letters [FR 41]

From Mr Curly to Vasco Pyjama (Circumnavigator)

Dear Vasco
It is the shortest day here in Curly Flat — the winter
solstice. We had a very interesting time trying to measure
this shortest day. How does one measure a day? Length is
one matter, but depth and width are just as important.
For instance, a short day may be very deep or a long day
may be shallow and narrow. What seems to be vital is
whether or not the day is spacious, in which case the
roundedness of the day is perhaps the most important
factor. After all, a round day holds happiness most successfully — happiness itself being of a rounded shape, as
you have observed.

The shortest day always reminds me that life is short,
but no sooner am I conscious of that than I am reminded
that life is also very long. This is a most comforting
paradox, for when I know that it is short, life seems more
precious and sweet; I am overcome with a great sense of
forgiveness and my sufferings seem more bearable and
fleeting — in fact they almost feel like blessings.

And when I know that life is long I am reassured and contented that the great wheel will surely turn and natural justice will come to pass most certainly. But once again, it is not the length of life which is important, it is the shape and the spaciousness — for therein lies the potential for a beautiful freedom. It is the roundness of life which matters. A round life is surely a happy life — and dare I say — it is a good life.

Michael Leunig (The Age)

I have included the following two readings in what is a secular and cultural collection because many non-church people request them for their traditional or cultured value. Other families choose to include these readings out of respect to those attending who may be Jewish or Christian.

The Lord's Prayer [FR 42]

Our Father, who art in heaven,
Hallowed be thy name,
Thy kingdom come,
Thy will be done
On earth as it is in heaven.

Give us this day
Our daily bread,
And forgive us our trespasses
As we forgive those who trespass against us.

And lead us not into temptation,
But deliver us from evil,
For thine is the kingdom,
The power and the glory,
Forever and ever.
Amen.

The Lord Is My Shepherd [FR 43]

The Lord is my shepherd;
there is nothing I shall want.
Fresh and green are the pastures
Where he gives me repose,
Near restful waters he leads me
to revive my drooping spirit,
He guides me along the right path;
He is true to his name.
If I should walk in the valley of the shadow of death
No evil would I fear,
You are there with your crook and your staff,
with these you give me comfort.
You have prepared a banquet for me
in the sight of my foes,
My head you have anointed with oil,
My cup is overflowing.

Surely goodness and kindness follow me
All the days of my life;
In the lord's own house shall I dwell
Forever and ever.

The Committal

(Celebrant, Jan Brown)

AGNES [FC 6]

Celebrant:

Tenderly, lovingly and reverently,
we commit the body of *Agnes Mary Prince*
to nature's keeping.

We give thanks for her life,
we remember with gratitude her deep love for her
    family,
her sense of fun and her generous heart.

May any regrets we feel today be turned into gratitude
for the time we shared with *Agnes*.
And may the chill of darkness of death give way to the
warmth and sunshine of her memory that we will
cherish forever.

May we leave this place in the quietness of *Agnes's*
memory,
offering our love and support to her family.

Interment of Ashes

JONATHAN   [FI I]

If the ashes are interred in a burial plot, the family may wish to
have a further brief ceremony such as this, followed by some
readings.

Celebrant:

In placing the ashes of *Jonathan Michael Rogers* in this
hallowed ground,
we think again of all that our dear companion and friend
meant and means to us.
We dedicate this simple plot, amid these natural
surroundings,
to every beautiful and precious memory associated with
him.

We lay these ashes in that gentle earth
that has been the chief support of humans
since first we walked beneath the sun.
To all human beings, to all living forms,
the soil has ever provided the sustenance
that is the staff of life.

To that good earth
we now commit the ashes of our friend,
and say, with the poet Shelley,
that you are now one with nature.

Bibliography and Further Readings

Barnes, Marian. *Funerals to Celebrate Life.* Simon & Schuster, East Roseville, NSW, 1992.

Batten, Juliet. *Celebrating the Southern Seasons.* Tandem Press, Birkenhead, NZ, 1995.

Carcopino, Jerome. *Daily Life in Ancient Rome.* Peregrine, London, 1970.

Day, Jane. *How to Perform Under Pressure.* Daybreak Press, Melbourne, 1995.

Dineen, Jacqueline. *Rites of Passage.* Chelsea House, London, 1998.

Gibran, Kahlil. *The Prophet.* William Heinemann, London, 1972.

Griffin, G. & Tobin, D. *In the Midst of Life.* Melbourne University Press, Melbourne, 1982.

Hocking, Jenny. *Lionel Murphy: A Political Biography.* Cambridge University Press, Cambridge, 1997; see the bibliography.

Hudson, Hilary. *Civil Rites and Ceremonies,* Heritage Press, Waikanae, NZ, 1996.

Jung, Carl G. *Man and His Symbols.* Penguin, London, 1964.

Kingma, D. R. *Weddings from the Heart.* Conari, Berkeley, Calif., 1991.

Kubler-Ross, Elizabeth. *Death: The Final Stage of Growth.* Prentice-Hall, Englewood Cliffs, New Jersey, 1975.

——. *On Death and Dying.* Macmillan, New York, 1969.

——. *Questions and Answers on Death and Dying.* Macmillan, New York, 1974.

——. *To Live Until We Say Goodbye.* Prentice-Hall, Englewood Cliffs, New Jersey, 1997.

Linder-Pelz, Susie. *Well Over Fifty.* Allen & Unwin, Sydney, 1991.

McKissock, Mal. *Coping with Grief.* ABC Enterprises, Sydney, 1984.

Macnab, Francis. *Life After Loss.* Millenium, Newtown, NSW, 1989.

Mahdi, L. C., Christopher, N., G., Meade, M. *Crossroads: The Quest for Contemporary Rites of Passage.* Open Court, Chicago, 1996 (mainly about adolescence).

Messenger, Dally R. *So, Mum and Dad Have Separated.* Dally M. Publishing & Research, Melbourne, 1997 (distributed by Ken Pryse, Melbourne).

Monserrat, Ann. *And the Bride Wore.* Hodder & Staughton/Coronet, London, 1975.

Mooney, Bel (ed.). *The Penguin Book of Marriage*. Penguin, London, 1989.

Mynott, Lawrence. *Classic Love Poems*. Chancellor, London, 1998.

The New Penguin Book of Love Poems. Penguin, Ringwood, Vic., 1988.

The Oxford Dictionary of Quotations. 2nd edn. Oxford University Press, Oxford, 1974.

The Penguin Book of Death. Penguin, Ringwood, Vic., 1997.

The Penguin Dictionary of Quotations. 2nd edn. Penguin, Ringwood, 1994.

Peters, Vlady M. *The Complete Book of Australian Weddings*. Kangaroo, Kenthurst, NSW, 1987.

Rinder, Walter. *Love Is an Attitude*. Celestial Arts, Berkeley, Calif., 1972.

St Aubyn, Lorna. *Rituals for Everyday Living*. Judy Piatkus, London, 1994.

Schillebeeckx, E. *Marriage: Secular Reality and Saving Mystery*, vols 1 and 11. Sheed & Ward/Stagbooks, London, 1965.

Scutt, J. (ed.). *Lionel Murphy: A Radical Judge*. McCulloch, Melbourne, 1987.

Strauss, Jennifer (ed.). *The Oxford Book of Australian Love Poems*. Oxford University Press, Melbourne, 1997.

Tease, J. *Wedding Daze*. Vivien Twyford Communications, Wollongong, NSW, 1990.

Van Gennep, Arnold. *Rites of Passage*. Routledge & Kegan Paul, London, 1960.

Venturini, G. (ed.). *Five Voices for Lionel*. Federation Press, Sydney, 1994.

Walter, Tony. *Funerals — and How to Improve Them*. Hodder & Staughton, London, 1990.

Weller, Shane. *Great Love Poems*, Dover, New York, 1992.

Willson, Jane W. *To Love and to Cherish: A Guide to Non-religious Wedding Ceremonies*. British Humanist Association, London, 1989.

Music and Songs

Musical is integral to almost every ceremony. Apart from the music mentioned throughout this book, here is an additional short list to stimulate your ideas on a choice of suitable music and songs.

Music/Song	Singer	Ceremony
Air, from *Water Music* (Handel)		Wedding (prelude)
Air on a G String (Bach)		Wedding (prelude)
All I Ask of You	Sarah Brightman/ Michael Crawford	Wedding
Amazing Grace		Funeral
Annie's Song	John Denver/ Placido Domingo	Wedding
Arrival of the Queen of Sheba (Handel)		Wedding (entrance)
Ave Maria (Gounod)	Luciano Pavarotti	Wedding
Ave Maria (Schubert)	Luciano Pavarotti	Wedding
Be My Love	Jose Carreras/ Mario Lanza	Wedding
Beautiful Boy	John Lennon	Naming
Because (Ebbinghouse)	Placido Domingo/ Mario Lanza	Wedding
Because You're Mine	Mario Lanza/ Nat King Cole	Wedding
Bridal Chorus, from *Lohengrin* (Wagner)		Wedding (entrance)
Can't Help Falling in Love	Elvis Presley	Wedding
Canon in D (Pachelbel)		Wedding (entrance)
Darling, Je vous aime beaucoup	Nat King Cole	Wedding
Diane	Donald Novis	Wedding/Funeral
Don't Fence Me In		Farewell/ Redundancy
For You	John Denver	Wedding
From This Moment On	Shania Twain	Wedding
Hornpipe in D, from *Water Music* (Handel)		Wedding (recessional)

Music/Song	Singer	Ceremony
If There's Anything That You Want	The Beatles	Wedding
I'll Get By as Long as I Have You		Wedding
I'll Take You Home Again, Kathleen		Wedding/Funeral
Jesu, Joy of Man's Desiring (Bach)		Wedding (prelude)
Largo (Handel)		Wedding (prelude)
Let Me Call You Sweetheart	Bing Crosby	Wedding/Funeral
Louise	Maurice Chevalier	Wedding/Funeral
Love Me Tender	Elvis Presley	Wedding
A Love Until the End of Time	Placido Domingo/ Maureen McGovern	Wedding
Maggie		Wedding /Funeral
Magnolia	John Marvin	Wedding/Funeral
Marry Me	Neil Diamond	Wedding
Nice Work If You Can Get It		Farewell/ Redundancy
One Hand, One Heart (Sondheim)	Kiri Te Kanawa	Wedding
Panis Angelicus	Luciano Pavarotti	Wedding
Perhaps Love	Placido Domingo/ John Denver	Wedding
Ramona	Gene Austin	Wedding/Funeral
Rose Marie	Nelson Eddy	Wedding/Funeral
Sally	Gracie Fields	Wedding/Funeral
Sheep May Safely Graze (Bach)		Weddings (prelude)
Sweet Sue, Just You	George Metaxa	Wedding/Funeral
Take That Job and Shove It		Farewell/ Redundancy
The More I See You	Nat King Cole	Wedding
Toccata (Widor)		Wedding (recessional)
Trumpet Tune and Air (Purcell)		Wedding (recessional)
Trumpet Voluntary (Clarke)		Wedding (entrance)
Unforgettable	Nat King Cole	Wedding
Wedding March (Mendelssohn)	Wedding	(recessional)

Music/Song	Singer	Ceremony
We'll Meet Again	Inkspots	Farewell/Funeral
When I Fall in Love	Nat King Cole	Wedding
When the Saints Come Marchin' In		Funeral
You Made Me Love You	Nat King Cole	Wedding
You're So Easy to Love	Anthony Warlow	Wedding

Index of Readings and Authors